Name _____     Date _____

# Activity: Numbers 0 Through 5

Count. Write the number.

1.     _ _ _ _ _ _ _ _ _ _
four

2. _____
_ _ _ _ _ _ _ _ _ _
zero

3.    _____
_ _ _ _ _ _ _ _ _ _
two

4. ☆ ☆ ☆
☆ ☆   _____
_ _ _ _ _ _ _ _ _ _
five

5. ▭ ▭ ▭   _____
_ _ _ _ _ _ _ _ _ _
three

6. ⬠   _____
_ _ _ _ _ _ _ _ _ _
one

---

**Test Prep**

Fill in the ○ for the correct answer. NH means Not Here.
How many shapes are there?

7. ♡ ♡ ♡

   five   four  three  NH
    ○      ○     ○     ○

8.

   0     3     5    NH
   ○      ○     ○     ○

Explain how you knew the correct answer.

_____

_____

**Use with text pages 7–8.**

Name _____ Date _____

# Activity: Numbers 6 Through 10

Count. Write the number.

1.

     9

nine

2.

six

3.

seven

4.

ten

5.

six

6.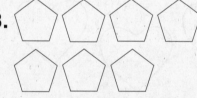

eight

## Test Prep

Fill in the ○ for the correct answer. NH means Not Here.
How many shapes are there?

7.

    seven   eight   nine   NH
       ○      ○     ○     ○

8.

     6    7   10   NH
    ○     ○     ○     ○

**Use with text pages 9–10.**

# Order 0 Through 10

Write the numbers. Use the number line.

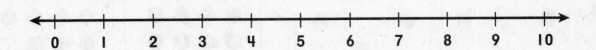

1. Just before

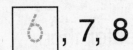
6 , 7, 8

☐ , 4, 5

2. Just after

8, 9, ☐

7, 8, ☐

3. Between

5, ☐ , 7

4, ☐ , 6

4. Just before and just after

☐ , 2, ☐

☐ , 7, ☐

---

**Test Prep**

Fill in the ○ for the correct answer. NH means Not Here.
Which number is missing?

5. 2, 3, 4, ☐

4    5    6    NH
○    ○    ○    ○

6. ☐ , 8, 9, 10

5    6    7    NH
○    ○    ○    ○

Explain how you knew which number to fill in.

_____

_____

**Use with text pages 11–12.**

Name _____ Date _____

# Compare 0 Through 10

Circle the words that make the sentence true.

1.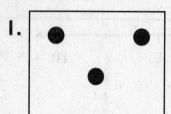

2.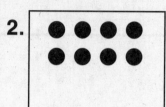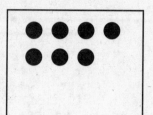

(3) is greater than / ~~is less than~~ 5

(8) ~~is greater than~~ / is less than 7

3. (10) ~~is greater than~~ / is less than 5

4. (4) is greater than / is less than 9

---

**Test Prep**

Fill in the ○ for the correct answer. NH means Not Here.

5. Which number is greater than 8?

   6    7    9    NH
   ○    ○    ●    ○

6. Which number is less than 4?

   8    6    4    NH
   ○    ○    ○    ●

Explain how you knew which number to fill in.

_____

_____

**Use with text pages 13–15.**

4

# Activity: Numbers 10 Through 15

Count. Write the number.

1.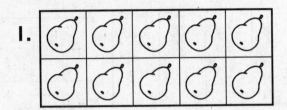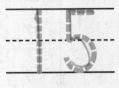

fifteen

2.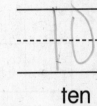

ten

3.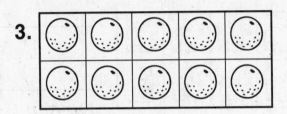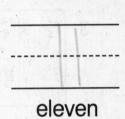

eleven

**Test Prep**

Fill in the ○ for the correct answer. NH means Not Here.

How many dots are there?

4.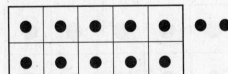

5.

| 13 | 15 | 17 | NH |    | 12 | 14 | 16 | NH |
|----|----|----|----|----|----|----|----|----|
| ● | ○ | ○ | ○ |    | ○ | ● | ○ | ○ |

**Use with text pages 17–18.**

5

# Activity: Numbers 16 Through 20

Count. Write the number.

**1.**

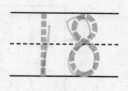

eighteen

**2.**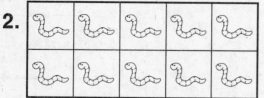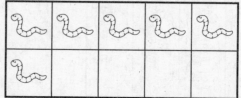

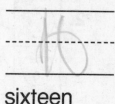

sixteen

**3.**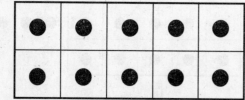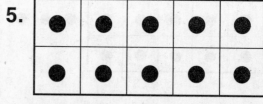

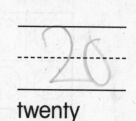

twenty

## Test Prep

Fill in the ○ for the correct answer. NH means Not Here.
How many dots are there?

**4.**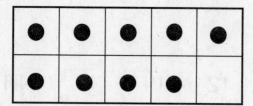

sixteen  nineteen  twenty  NH
○        ○         ○       ○

**5.**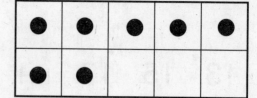

17   18   19   NH
○    ○    ○    ○

**Use with text pages 19–20.**

# Order 11 Through 20

Write the numbers. Use the number line.

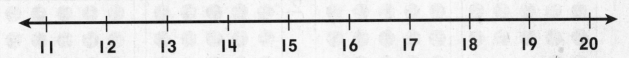

11    12    13    14    15    16    17    18    19    20

**1. Just after**

17, 18, __19__

14, 15, __16__

**2. Just before**

__11__, 12, 13

__15__, 16, 17

**3. Between**

11, __12__, 13

17, __18__, 19

**4. Just before and just after**

__18__, 19, __20__

__11__, 12, __13__

---

**Test Prep**

Fill in the ○ for the correct answer. NH means Not Here.
Which number is missing?

**5.** 12, 13, 14, [15]

14    15    16    NH
○    ◉    ○    ○

**6.** [17], 18, 19, 20

15    16    17    NH
○    ○    ◉    ○

**Use with text pages 21–22.**

# Compare 11 Through 20

Circle the words that make the sentence true.

1.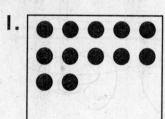

12    is greater than
      (is less than)    14

2.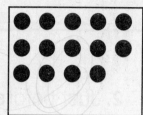

17    is less than
      is equal to    17

3.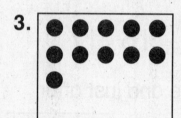

11    is greater than
      is less than    15

4.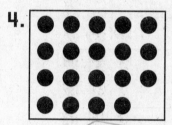

19    (is greater than)
      is less than    16

5.
13    is greater than
      is equal to    13

6.
17    is greater than
      is less than    18

---

## Test Prep

Fill in the ○ for the correct answer. NH means Not Here.

7. Which number is greater
   than 18?

   17    18    19    NH
   ○     ○     ◉     ○

8. Which number is less than
   15?

   11    15    16    NH
   ◉     ○     ○     ○

Use with text pages 23–24.

# Problem Solving:
# Draw a Picture

1. Marisa has 9 marbles.
Jean has 1 more.
How many marbles does
Jean have?

Jean has ___10___ marbles.

Draw or write to explain.

$$9 + 1 =$$

---

2. Ellen has 11 pennies.
She has 1 fewer dimes.
How many dimes does
she have?

Ellen has ___12___ dimes.

$$11 + 1 = 12$$

**Test Prep**

3. Fill in the ○ for the correct answer. NH means Not Here.

There are 6 rabbits.
There is the same number of
brown rabbits as white rabbits.
How many are white?

12     3     6     NH
○     ○     ◉     ○

Draw or write to solve.

**Use with text pages 25–27.**

Name _____ Date _____

# Activity: Addition Stories

Tell a story about 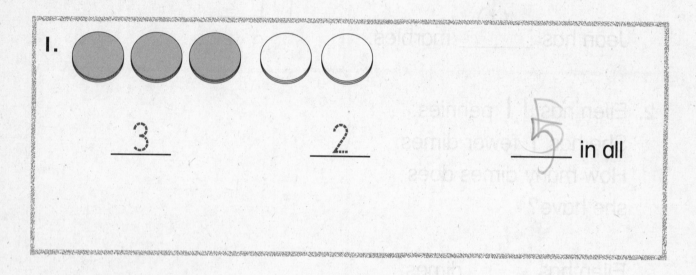 and .
You can use two different colored counters.
If you work with a partner you can each tell a
different part of the story.
Write the numbers.

I.

_3_          _2_          _5_ in all

**Test Prep**

Fill in the ○ for the correct answer. NH means Not Here.

2. Which set of counters shows 6?

○

○

○

NH
○

Copyright © Houghton Mifflin Company. All rights reserved.

**Use with text pages 35–36.**

10

Name _____ Date _____

# Model Addition

Use Workmat 3 and counters.

Show the parts. Find the whole.

1. 
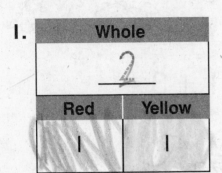

| Whole | |
|---|---|
| 2 | |
| Red | Yellow |
| I | I |

2. 

| Whole | |
|---|---|
| | |
| Red | Yellow |
| 3 | 2 |

**Test Prep**

Fill in the ○ for the correct answer. NH means Not Here.

3. Find the whole.

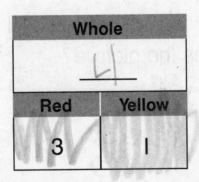

| Whole | |
|---|---|
| 4 | |
| Red | Yellow |
| 3 | I |

| 3 | 5 | 4 | NH |
|---|---|---|---|
| ○ | ○ | ◉ | ○ |

Explain how you used the counters to add.

_____

_____

**Use with text pages 37–38.**

# Use Symbols to Add

Write the sum.

1.

$2 + 3 = \underline{5}$

2.

$1 + 3 = \underline{4}$

3.

$2 + 4 = \underline{\phantom{6}}$

4.

$3 + 1 = \underline{4}$

**Test Prep**

5. Fill in the ○ for the correct answer. NH means Not Here.

Which sum matches the picture?

$5 + 1 = \boxed{?}$

| 4 | 3 | 6 | NH |
|---|---|---|---|
| ○ | ○ | ○ | ○ |

Explain how you found the sum of 5 and 1.

_____

_____

**Use with text pages 39–40.**

# Add With Zero

Write the sum.

1. $2 + 0 =$ __2__     2. $2 + 4 =$ __6__     3. $1 + 5 =$ __6__

4. $2 + 3 =$ __5__     5. $0 + 1 =$ __1__     6. $5 + 0 =$ __5__

7. $0 + 3 =$ __3__     8. $4 + 0 =$ __4__     9. $1 + 4 =$ __5__

10. $3 + 3 =$ __6__     11. $2 + 4 =$ __6__     12. $6 + 0 =$ __6__

**Test Prep**

Fill in the ○ for the correct answer. NH means Not Here.

13. $0 + 5 =$ ?

0     3     5     NH
○     ○     ○     ○

Explain what happened when you added 0 and 5.

_____

_____

**Use with text pages 41–42.**

Practice 2.5

# Add in Any Order

Use cubes. Make the train. Complete the addition sentences.

**1.** Make a **5** train.

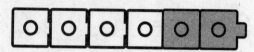

$\underline{2} + \underline{3} = \underline{5}$

$\underline{3} + \underline{2} = \underline{5}$

**2.** Make a **6** train.

$\underline{\phantom{0}} + \underline{\phantom{0}} = \underline{\phantom{0}}$

$\underline{\phantom{0}} + \underline{\phantom{0}} = \underline{\phantom{0}}$

Add. Then change the order of the addends and add.

**3.** $5 + 1 = \underline{6}$

$\underline{1} + \underline{5} = \underline{6}$

**4.** $4 + 1 = \underline{5}$

$\underline{1} + \underline{4} = \underline{5}$

**5.** $2 + 0 = \underline{2}$

$\underline{0} + \underline{2} = \underline{2}$

**6.** $2 + 3 = \underline{5}$

$\underline{3} + \underline{2} = \underline{5}$

### Test Prep

Fill in the ○ for the correct answer. NH means Not Here.

**7.** $2 + 1 = 3$     $1 + 2 = ?$

    3     0     2    NH

    ●     ○     ○    ○

**Use with text pages 45–46.**

Name _____ Date _____

# Ways to Make Numbers

Use two colors to show a way to make 7.
Complete the addition sentence.

1.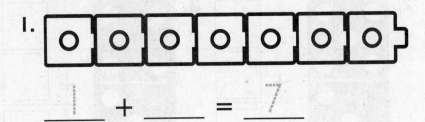

_____ + _____ = _____ 7

Use two colors to show a way to make 8.
Complete the addition sentence.

2.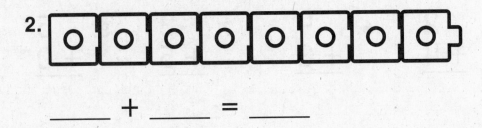

_____ + _____ = _____

**Test Prep**

Fill in the ○ for the correct answer. NH means Not Here.

3. $5 + 2 = ?$

5     7     4     NH
○     ○     ○     ○

Explain your answer.

**Use with text pages 47–48.**

# Add in Vertical Form

Complete the addition fact.

1.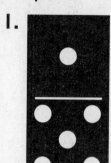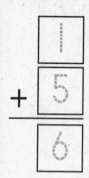

2.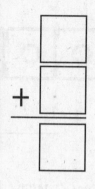

3.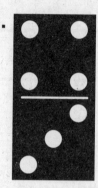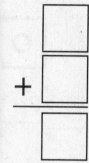

Write the sum.

4.    3
   + 2

5.    2
   + 4

6.    4
   + 3

7.    3
   + 5

8.    5
   + 0

---

**Test Prep**

Fill in the ○ for the correct answer. NH means Not Here.

9.    1
   + 7

    7    6    8    NH
    ○    ○    ○     ○

Explain how adding across and adding down are the same.

_____

**Use with text pages 49–50.**

Name _____ Date _____

# Problem Solving:
# Write a Number Sentence

Write the addition sentence.
Write the answer.

1.

   $4 \; (+) \; 2 \; (=) \; 6$

   There are 4 rabbits eating.
   Then 2 more rabbits come.
   How many rabbits in all?  ___6___ rabbits

2.

   ___ ◯ ___ ◯ ___

   There are 3 butterflies.
   Then 4 butterflies join them.
   How many butterflies in all?  _____ butterflies

**Test Prep**

Fill in the ○ for the correct answer. NH means Not Here.

3.

   $4 + 4 = \, ?$

   There are 4 bugs on a leaf.
   Then 4 bugs join them.
   How many bugs in all?

   8        4        6        NH
   ○        ○        ○        ○

**Use with text pages 51–53.**

# Activity: Subtraction Stories

**1.** Ethan saw 4 birds in the bird bath.

One of the birds flew away.

Use counters to show the story and write the numbers.

_____    _____ flew away    _____ are left

**Test Prep**

Fill in the ○ for the correct answer. NH means Not Here.

**2.** $1 + 3 = \boxed{\phantom{0}}$

    4           3           2          NH

    ○           ○           ○          ○

**Use with text pages 61–62.**

# Model Subtraction

Use Workmat 3 and counters.

Show the whole. Move the counters to one part.

Find the other part.

**1.**

| Whole |
|:---:|
| 4 |

| Part | Part |
|:---:|:---:|
| 3 | ___ |

**2.**

| Whole |
|:---:|
| 5 |

| Part | Part |
|:---:|:---:|
| 1 | ___ |

**3.**

| Whole |
|:---:|
| 3 |

| Part | Part |
|:---:|:---:|
| 1 | ___ |

**4.**

| Whole |
|:---:|
| 4 |

| Part | Part |
|:---:|:---:|
| 2 | ___ |

### Test Prep

Fill in the ○ for the correct answer. NH means Not Here.

**5.** There are 5 birds. Then 2 birds join them.

How many birds in all?

3    5    7    NH
○    ○    ○    ○

**Use with text pages 63–64.**

Name _____ Date _____

Practice
3.3

# Use Symbols to Subtract

Circle and cross out to subtract.

Write how many are left.

1.

5 − 1 = __4__

2.

6 − 2 = ____

3. 

4 − 3 = ____

4.

6 − 3 = ____

**Test Prep**

Fill in the ○ for the correct answer. NH means Not Here.

5. Allen has 4 🌼. He gives 2 away.
   How many does he have left?

4   3   2   NH
○   ○   ○   ○

Explain how you got the answer.

_____

_____

**Use with text pages 65–66.**

# Write Subtraction Sentences

Write the subtraction sentence.

1. _6_ ◯ _3_ ◯ _3_

2. ___ ◯ ___ ◯ ___

3. ___ ◯ ___ ◯ ___

4. ___ ◯ ___ ◯ ___

Write the difference.

5. $5 - 4 =$ _____   6. $5 - 3 =$ _____   7. $3 - 2 =$ _____

8. $6 - 2 =$ _____   9. $2 - 1 =$ _____   10. $4 - 3 =$ _____

### Test Prep

Fill in the ○ for the correct answer. NH means Not Here.

11. There are 6 🙂 on the team. Then 1 🙂 goes home.
    How many 🙂 are still playing?

    2        7        4        NH
    ○        ○        ○        ○

Explain how you arrived at your answer.

**Use with text pages 67–68.**

# Zero in Subtraction

Write the difference.

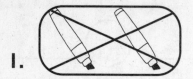

**1.**

$$2 - 2 = \underline{\quad}$$

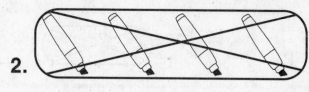

**2.**

$$4 - 4 = \underline{\quad}$$

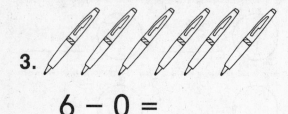

**3.**

$$6 - 0 = \underline{\quad}$$

**4.**

$$3 - 3 = \underline{\quad}$$

**5.** $1 - 1 = \underline{\quad}$  |  **6.** $3 - 0 = \underline{\quad}$  |  **7.** $5 - 5 = \underline{\quad}$

**8.** $2 - 0 = \underline{\quad}$  |  **9.** $6 - 6 = \underline{\quad}$  |  **10.** $1 - 0 = \underline{\quad}$

**Test Prep**

Fill in the ○ for the correct answer. NH means Not Here.

**11.** Martin has 5 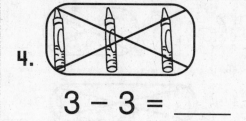. He doesn't lose any of them.
How many does he have left?

0        1        5        NH
○        ○        ○        ○

Explain what happens when you subtract zero
from a number.

_____

_____

**Use with text pages 71–72.**

# Subtract from 8 or Less

Use 8 cubes. Snap off some.
Circle and cross out the ones you snapped off.
Write the subtraction sentence.

1.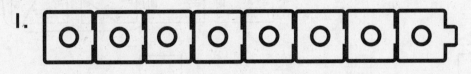

_____ – _____ = _____

2. 

_____ – _____ = _____

3. 

_____ – _____ = _____

---

**Test Prep**

Fill in the ○ for the correct answer. NH means Not Here.

4. Ed makes a tower with 8 blocks.
   Then 3 fall off.
   How many blocks are left?

   8       4       3       NH
   ○       ○       ○       ○

**Use with text pages 73–74.**

# Subtract in Vertical Form

Complete the subtraction fact.

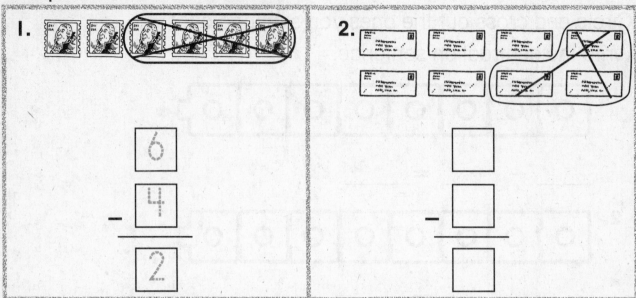

1.
$$\begin{array}{r} 6 \\ -\ 4 \\ \hline 2 \end{array}$$

2.
$$\begin{array}{r} \square \\ -\ \square \\ \hline \square \end{array}$$

Write the difference.

| 3. | 4. | 5. | 6. | 7. | 8. |
|---|---|---|---|---|---|
| $\begin{array}{r}7\\-7\\\hline\end{array}$ | $\begin{array}{r}3\\-0\\\hline\end{array}$ | $\begin{array}{r}4\\-2\\\hline\end{array}$ | $\begin{array}{r}3\\-2\\\hline\end{array}$ | $\begin{array}{r}5\\-5\\\hline\end{array}$ | $\begin{array}{r}2\\-2\\\hline\end{array}$ |

**Test Prep**

Fill in the ○ for the correct answer. NH means Not Here.

9. Find the difference.

$$\begin{array}{r} 7 \\ -\ 6 \\ \hline \end{array}$$

| 7 | 1 | 5 | NH |
|---|---|---|---|
| ○ | ○ | ○ | ○ |

**Use with text pages 75–76.**

Name _____ Date _____

# Problem Solving:
# Act It Out With Models

Act out the problem with counters.
Write the answer.

1. Joanne has 7 party
   balloons. Then 3 balloons
   pop. How many balloons
   are left?

   ___4___ balloons

2. Beth has 8 party hats
   and 2 hats are blue.
   How many hats are
   not blue?

   _____ hats

Draw or write to explain.

**Test Prep**

Fill in the ○ for the correct answer. NH means Not Here.

3. James gets 6 presents. He opens 3 of them.
   How many presents are unopened?

   9       5       3       NH
   ○       ○       ○       ○

Use with text pages 77–79.

Name _____ Date _____

# Activity: Make a Tally Chart

1. Use the picture. Complete the tally chart. Cross out a picture and write **I** tally mark for each animal you cross out.

Use the tally chart to solve.

| | Animals |
|---|---|
| | I I I |
| | |
| | |

2. How many  are there?

   _____

3. How many  are there?

   _____

4. Which has the most? Circle.

5. Which has the fewest? Circle.

**Test Prep**

Fill in the ○ for the correct answer. NH means Not Here.

6. How many  and are there in all?

   I I     8     5     NH
   ○      ○      ○       ○

**Use with text pages 87–88.**

# Read a Pictograph

| Fruit Children Like | |
|---|---|
| 🍎 | 👦👦👦👦👦👦👦 |
| 🍌 | 👦👦👦👦 |
| 🍊 | 👦👦👦👦 |

Use the pictograph to solve.
Each 👦 stands for 1 child.

1. How many children like 🍌?

   __4__ children

2. Which fruit do most children like? Circle.

   🍌   🍎   🍊

3. Which two fruits do the same number of children like? Circle.

         🍊

4. How many children like 🍌 and ?

   _____ children

**Test Prep**

Fill in the ○ for the correct answer. NH means Not Here.

5. How many children like apples?

   7        8        11        NH
   ○        ○        ○         ○

**Use with text pages 89–90.**

27

# Make a Pictograph

1. Use the picture. Make a pictograph.

| | Toys |
|---|---|
| 🧸 | 😊 😊 😊 😊 |
| 🐘 | |
| 🐢 | |

Use the pictograph to solve.

2. How many more 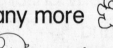 than 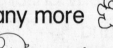 are there?

_____ more

3. How many 🐘 and 🐢 are there?

_____

**Test Prep**

Fill in the ○ for the correct answer. NH means Not Here.

4. How many 🧸 and 🐘 are there in all?

| 10 | 6 | 8 | NH |
|---|---|---|---|
| ○ | ○ | ○ | ○ |

**Use with text pages 91–93.**

# Read a Bar Graph

The bar graph shows
how many children
have each kind of pet.

**Pets We Have**

Number of Children

**Kinds of Pets**

Use the bar graph to solve.

1. Circle the pet 3 children
   have.

2. Do fewer children have
    or ? Circle.

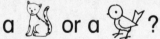

3. How many children have
   a  or a ?

   _____

4. How many more children
   have 🐶 than 🐦?

   _____ more

**Test Prep**

Fill in the ○ for the correct answer. NH means Not Here.

5. If 1 more child had a cat, how many
   children would have cats?

   4        5        6        NH
   ○        ○        ○        ○

Use with text pages 95–96.

# Activity: Make a Bar Graph

**1.** Use the picture. Make a bar graph.

**Favorite Sports**

| Kinds of Sports | 0 | 1 | 2 | 3 | 4 | 5 | 6 | 7 |
|---|---|---|---|---|---|---|---|---|
| 🚴 | | | | | | | | |
| 🏊 | | | | | | | | |
| 🔭 | | | | | | | | |
| 🚶 | | | | | | | | |

**Number of people**

Use the bar graph to solve.

**2.** How many more 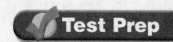 than 🔭 are there?

_____ more

## Test Prep

Fill in the ○ for the correct answer. NH means Not Here.

**3.** How many 🔭 and 🚴 are there?

3       7       2       NH
○       ○       ○       ○

**Use with text pages 97–99.**

# Problem Solving: Use a Graph

Use the bar graph to solve.

**Books We Have Read**

| | 0 | 1 | 2 | 3 | 4 | 5 | 6 | 7 |
|---|---|---|---|---|---|---|---|---|
| Dinosaur Dig | | | | | | | | |
| The Silly School | | | | | | | | |
| My Mysteries | | | | | | | | |

**Number of Children**

---

1. How many more children read *Dinosaur Dig* than *The Silly School*?

   __2__ more children

   Draw or write to explain.

2. How many children in all read either *Dinosaur Dig* or *The Silly School*?

   _____ in all

---

**Test Prep**

Fill in the ○ for the correct answer. NH means Not Here.

3. How many more children would have to read *Dinosaur Dig* to have the same number as *My Mysteries*?

   1    3    4    NH
   ○    ○    ○    ○

**Use with text pages 101–103.**

Name _____ Date _____

# Count On to Add

Count on to add.

1. 5 + 3 = __8__          2. 6 + 1 = _____

3. 7 + 3 = _____     4. 5 + 2 = _____     5. 8 + 1 = _____

6.  7      7.  6      8.  5      9.  4      10.  8      11.  4
   + 1        + 3        + 1        + 2         + 2         + 1

12.  3     13.  2     14.  6     15.  3     16.  6     17.  7
   + 1        + 3        + 4        + 2         + 2         + 2

**Test Prep**

Fill in the ○ for the correct answer. NH means Not Here.

18. 4 puppies are inside.

   How many puppies are there?

   6      5      4      NH
   ○      ○      ○      ○

Explain how you got your answer.

_____

_____

**Use with text pages 125–126.**

# Use a Number Line to Add

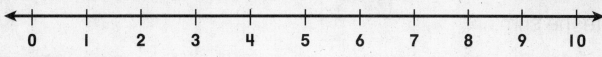

```
0   1   2   3   4   5   6   7   8   9   10
```

Find the sum.

1. $4 + 2 = \underline{6}$   2. $6 + 1 = \underline{\phantom{0}}$   3. $8 + 2 = \underline{\phantom{0}}$

4. $5 + 3 = \underline{\phantom{0}}$   5. $2 + 1 = \underline{\phantom{0}}$   6. $7 + 2 = \underline{\phantom{0}}$

7.  $\begin{array}{r} 5 \\ +2 \\ \hline \end{array}$
8.  $\begin{array}{r} 6 \\ +3 \\ \hline \end{array}$
9.  $\begin{array}{r} 1 \\ +7 \\ \hline \end{array}$
10. $\begin{array}{r} 3 \\ +5 \\ \hline \end{array}$
11. $\begin{array}{r} 8 \\ +1 \\ \hline \end{array}$
12. $\begin{array}{r} 7 \\ +3 \\ \hline \end{array}$

13. $\begin{array}{r} 2 \\ +7 \\ \hline \end{array}$
14. $\begin{array}{r} 5 \\ +1 \\ \hline \end{array}$
15. $\begin{array}{r} 3 \\ +6 \\ \hline \end{array}$
16. $\begin{array}{r} 4 \\ +3 \\ \hline \end{array}$
17. $\begin{array}{r} 6 \\ +2 \\ \hline \end{array}$
18. $\begin{array}{r} 3 \\ +7 \\ \hline \end{array}$

## Test Prep

Fill in the ○ for the correct answer. NH means Not Here.

19. Carrie wants to add $2 + 6$.
    What is the sum?

    30      7      8      NH
    ○       ○      ○      ○

**Explain your answer.** What number should Carrie count
on from? Why?

_____

_____

Use with text pages 127–128.

# Use Doubles to Add

Write the sum.

1. $2 + 2 = \underline{4}$  2. $5 + 5 = \underline{\quad}$  3. $4 + 4 = \underline{\quad}$

4. $3 + 3 = \underline{\quad}$  5. $4 + 4 = \underline{\quad}$  6. $1 + 1 = \underline{\quad}$

| 7. | 8. | 9. | 10. | 11. | 12. |
|---|---|---|---|---|---|
| $\begin{array}{r} 5 \\ +3 \\ \hline \end{array}$ | $\begin{array}{r} 6 \\ +2 \\ \hline \end{array}$ | $\begin{array}{r} 1 \\ +8 \\ \hline \end{array}$ | $\begin{array}{r} 0 \\ +0 \\ \hline \end{array}$ | $\begin{array}{r} 2 \\ +2 \\ \hline \end{array}$ | $\begin{array}{r} 1 \\ +1 \\ \hline \end{array}$ |

| 13. | 14. | 15. | 16. | 17. | 18. |
|---|---|---|---|---|---|
| $\begin{array}{r} 2 \\ +5 \\ \hline \end{array}$ | $\begin{array}{r} 5 \\ +5 \\ \hline \end{array}$ | $\begin{array}{r} 6 \\ +3 \\ \hline \end{array}$ | $\begin{array}{r} 4 \\ +4 \\ \hline \end{array}$ | $\begin{array}{r} 6 \\ +0 \\ \hline \end{array}$ | $\begin{array}{r} 3 \\ +6 \\ \hline \end{array}$ |

## Test Prep

Fill in the ○ for the correct answer.
NH means Not Here.

19. Jason has 3 pens.
    Alice has 3 pens.
    How many pens do they have?

    3   6   8   NH
    ○   ○   ○   ○

**Use with text pages 129–131.**

Name _____ Date _____

# Using Addition Strategies

Write the sum.

| 1. | 1<br>+ 3 | 2. | 4<br>+ 5 | 3. | 2<br>+ 8 | 4. | 9<br>+ 0 | 5. | 7<br>+ 2 | 6. | 3<br>+ 2 |

| 7. | 3<br>+ 5 | 8. | 6<br>+ 4 | 9. | 6<br>+ 3 | 10. | 1<br>+ 3 | 11. | 8<br>+ 0 | 12. | 5<br>+ 5 |

13. $5 + 3 =$ ____   14. $7 + 1 =$ ____   15. $2 + 7 =$ ____

16. $6 + 2 =$ ____   17. $4 + 5 =$ ____   18. $6 + 0 =$ ____

## Test Prep

Fill in the ○ for the correct answer. NH means Not Here.

19. Mom has 5 stamps. She buys 2 more.
    How many stamps does she have now?

    3        7        8        NH
    ○        ○        ○        ○

Explain how you found the answer.

_____

_____

**Use with text pages 133–134.**

# Problem Solving:
# Write a Number Sentence

Use Workmat 3 and counters.
Write a number sentence to solve.

1. The Tigers score 2 runs.
   The Bears score 3 runs.
   How many runs are
   there altogether?

   ___ ◯ ___ ◯ ___

   ___ runs

2. Alice has 4 stickers.
   Jenna has 4 stickers.
   How many stickers are
   there in all?

   ___ ◯ ___ ◯ ___

   ___ stickers

**Test Prep**

Fill in the ◯ for the correct answer. NH means Not Here.

3. There are 5 girls and 5 boys on the team.
   How many children are on the team?

   9    0    10    NH
   ◯    ◯    ◯     ◯

Explain how you found the answer.

_____

_____

Use with text pages 135–137.

Name _____ Date _____

# Count Back to Subtract

Count back to subtract.

1. $7 - 3 =$ ____      2. $9 - 2 =$ ____

3. $8 - 3 =$ ____   4. $10 - 1 =$ ____   5. $6 - 2 =$ ____

6. $9 - 3 =$ ____   7. $8 - 2 =$ ____   8. $10 - 3 =$ ____

9.  $\begin{array}{r} 10 \\ -\ 2 \\ \hline \end{array}$   10.  $\begin{array}{r} 5 \\ -\ 2 \\ \hline \end{array}$   11.  $\begin{array}{r} 7 \\ -\ 2 \\ \hline \end{array}$   12.  $\begin{array}{r} 8 \\ -\ 1 \\ \hline \end{array}$   13.  $\begin{array}{r} 5 \\ -\ 3 \\ \hline \end{array}$

14.  $\begin{array}{r} 5 \\ -\ 1 \\ \hline \end{array}$   15.  $\begin{array}{r} 7 \\ -\ 1 \\ \hline \end{array}$   16.  $\begin{array}{r} 4 \\ -\ 3 \\ \hline \end{array}$   17.  $\begin{array}{r} 3 \\ -\ 1 \\ \hline \end{array}$   18.  $\begin{array}{r} 10 \\ -\ 3 \\ \hline \end{array}$

## Test Prep

Fill in the ○ for the correct answer. NH means Not Here.

19. Subtract.   $\begin{array}{r} 10 \\ -\ 3 \\ \hline \end{array}$

    8     7     6     NH
    ○     ○     ○     ○

Explain how counting back helped you find the answer.

_____

Use with text pages 145–146.

# Use a Number Line to Subtract

Write the difference.

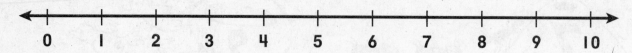

1. 7 − 2 = __5__   2. 6 − 3 = ____

3. 9 − 1 = ____   4. 5 − 2 = ____

5. 4 − 1 = ____   6. 6 − 2 = ____

7.  10   8.  5   9.  7   10.  8   11.  5
  − 2     − 2     − 2     − 1     − 3

12.  4   13.  10   14.  5   15.  6   16.  10
  − 3     − 1      − 3     − 1      − 3

**Test Prep**

Fill in the ○ for the correct answer. NH means Not Here.

17. Subtract.
        9
      − 2

   5     6     7     NH
   ○     ○     ○     ○

**Use with text pages 147–148.**

Name _____ Date _____

# How Many More? How Many Fewer?

Match. Then subtract.

1. How many more
   than ?

   $9 - 6 =$ __3__

2. How many fewer
   than ?

   $8 - 3 =$ ____

3. How many more
   than ?

   $10 - 6 =$ ____

4. How many more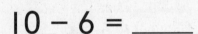
   than ?

   $7 - 2 =$ ____

**Test Prep**

Fill in the ○ for the correct answer. NH means Not Here.

5. Subtract.   7
             – 5

   3      2      1      NH
   ○      ○      ○      ○

Explain how matching helped
you find how many more or how
many fewer.

_____

_____

Use with text pages 149–151.

Name _____ Date _____

# Relate Addition and Subtraction

Use ⬜, ⬛, and Workmat 3.

Show the parts. Complete the related facts.

**1.**

| Whole |
| :---: |
| ? |

| Part | Part |
| :---: | :---: |

$6 + 3 =$ __9__

$9 - 3 =$ __6__

**2.**

| Whole |
| :---: |
| ? |

| Part | Part |
| :---: | :---: |

$2 + 5 =$ ___

$7 - 2 =$ ___

---

**3.** $6 + 2 =$ ___

$8 - 2 =$ ___

**4.** $5 + 3 =$ ___

$8 - 3 =$ ___

**5.** $2 + 7 =$ ___

$9 - 7 =$ ___

---

**6.** $1 + 3 =$ ___

$4 - 3 =$ ___

**7.** $8 + 2 =$ ___

$10 - 2 =$ ___

**8.** $4 + 4 =$ ___

$8 - 4 =$ ___

## Test Prep

Fill in the ○ for the correct answer.

NH means Not Here.

**9.** Which set of numbers shows the
related facts?

| Whole | |
| :---: | :---: |
| **Part** | **Part** |

$6 + 2 = 8$    $7 + 3 = 10$    $4 + 5 = 9$

$9 - 3 = 6$    $9 - 2 = 7$    $9 - 5 = 4$    NH

   ○       ○       ○       ○

**Use with text pages 153–154.**

# Fact Families

Use , and Workmat 3. Complete the fact family.

**1.**

| Whole |
|-------|
| 7 |

| Part | Part |
|------|------|
| 4 | 3 |

4 + 3 = 7    7 − 3 = 4

3 + 4 = 7    7 − 4 = 3

**2.**

| Whole |
|-------|
| 8 |

| Part | Part |
|------|------|
| 5 | 3 |

___ + ___ = ___    ___ − ___ = ___

___ + ___ = ___    ___ − ___ = ___

**3.**

| Whole |
|-------|
| 10 |

| Part | Part |
|------|------|
| 6 | 4 |

___ + ___ = ___    ___ − ___ = ___

___ + ___ = ___    ___ − ___ = ___

**4.**

| Whole |
|-------|
| 6 |

| Part | Part |
|------|------|
| 4 | 2 |

___ + ___ = ___    ___ − ___ = ___

___ + ___ = ___    ___ − ___ = ___

**Test Prep**

Fill in the ○ for the correct answer.

**5.** Which set of numbers shows the related facts?

| | | | Whole |
|---|---|---|-------|
| 5 + 2 = 7 | 3 + 3 = 6 | 1 + 7 = 8 | 7 |
| 2 + 5 = 7 | 2 + 3 = 5 | 7 + 2 = 9 | Part \| Part |
| 7 − 2 = 5 | 5 − 2 = 3 | 8 − 7 = 1 | 5 \| 2 |
| 7 − 5 = 2 | 6 − 3 = 3 | 9 − 2 = 7 | |
| ○ | ○ | ○ | |

**Use with text pages 155–156.**

Name _____ Date _____

# Using Subtraction Strategies

Write the difference.

| Ways to Subtract |
| --- |
| Count back. Use counters. Use a related addition fact. |

1. $4 - 0 =$ __4__

2. $7 - 2 =$ ___

3. $9 - 6 =$ ___

4. $5 - 4 =$ ___

5. $8 - 6 =$ ___

6. $6 - 4 =$ ___

7.
$$\begin{array}{r} 5 \\ -5 \\ \hline \end{array}$$

8.
$$\begin{array}{r} 8 \\ -5 \\ \hline \end{array}$$

9.
$$\begin{array}{r} 10 \\ -10 \\ \hline \end{array}$$

10.
$$\begin{array}{r} 4 \\ -3 \\ \hline \end{array}$$

11.
$$\begin{array}{r} 7 \\ -3 \\ \hline \end{array}$$

12.
$$\begin{array}{r} 6 \\ -5 \\ \hline \end{array}$$

13.
$$\begin{array}{r} 7 \\ -4 \\ \hline \end{array}$$

14.
$$\begin{array}{r} 6 \\ -3 \\ \hline \end{array}$$

15.
$$\begin{array}{r} 10 \\ -9 \\ \hline \end{array}$$

16.
$$\begin{array}{r} 8 \\ -3 \\ \hline \end{array}$$

17.
$$\begin{array}{r} 6 \\ -1 \\ \hline \end{array}$$

18.
$$\begin{array}{r} 9 \\ -9 \\ \hline \end{array}$$

19.
$$\begin{array}{r} 9 \\ -5 \\ \hline \end{array}$$

20.
$$\begin{array}{r} 10 \\ -0 \\ \hline \end{array}$$

21.
$$\begin{array}{r} 3 \\ -1 \\ \hline \end{array}$$

22.
$$\begin{array}{r} 9 \\ -7 \\ \hline \end{array}$$

23.
$$\begin{array}{r} 4 \\ -2 \\ \hline \end{array}$$

24.
$$\begin{array}{r} 8 \\ -7 \\ \hline \end{array}$$

## Test Prep

Fill in the ○ for the correct answer. NH means Not Here.

25. Subtract.
$$\begin{array}{r} 10 \\ -6 \\ \hline \end{array}$$
    10 ○    5 ○    4 ○    3 ○    NH ○

Explain how you found $10 - 6$.

_____

**Use with text pages 157–158.**

# Problem Solving:
# Choose the Operation

Choose the operation to solve.

1. There were 7 puppies sleeping. 4 puppies woke up. How many puppies were still sleeping?

Draw or write to explain.

__3__ puppies

2. 3 kittens play with a ball. 4 more come to play. How many kittens are playing now?

_____ kittens

3. The dog herded 3 cows from one field. Then it herded 5 cows from another field. How many cows did the dog herd in?

_____ cows

**Test Prep**

Fill in the ○ for the correct answer. NH means Not Here.

4. There are 8 puppy treats. 3 of the treats are eaten. How many puppy treats are left?

3          4          5          NH
○          ○          ○          ○

**Use with text pages 159–161.**

Name _____ Date _____

# Classifying and Sorting Objects

Tell how the shells are alike.
Write color, size, or shape.

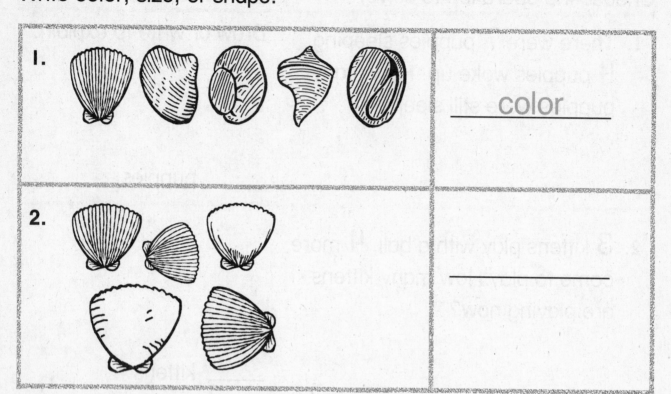

| | |
|---|---|
| 1. | _____color_____ |
| 2. | _____ |

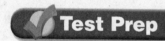 **Test Prep**

Fill in the ○ for the correct answer. NH means Not Here.

3.

Which bead belongs in the group above?

○   ◯   ▦   ▲   NH
    ○    ○    ○    ○

**Use with text pages 183–184.**

Name _____ Date _____

# Plane Shapes

1. Color the triangles ⟨ Red ⟩ .

2. Color the circles ⟨ Black ⟩ .

3. Color the square ⟨ Blue ⟩ .

4. Color the rectangles ⟨ Yellow ⟩ .

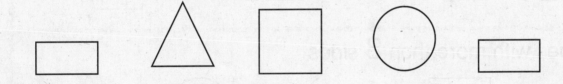

**Test Prep**

Fill in the ○ for the correct answer. NH means Not Here.

5. Which shape has **3** sides and **3** corners?

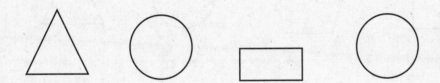

    ○         ○         ○         ○

**Use with text pages 185–186.**

Name _____ Date _____

# Classifying and Sorting Shapes

Read the sorting rule.
Circle the shapes that follow each rule.

1. Shapes with corners

2. Shapes with 3 corners

3. Shapes with more than 3 sides

**Test Prep**

Fill in the ○ for the correct answer. NH means Not Here.

4. Adam made a group of these shapes.

What was his sorting rule?

Large shapes      Small shapes      Square shapes          NH
     ○                   ○                 ○                  ○

Use with text pages 187–188.

46

# Activity: Solid Shapes

Circle the solid that matches.

**1. 0 edges**

**2. 5 faces**

Complete the table. Use solid shapes.
Write the number of faces, edges, and corners.

| | Number of Faces | Number of Edges | Number of Corners |
|---|---|---|---|
| **3.** cube | 6 | 12 | 8 |
| **4.** sphere | | | |
| **5.** cylinder | | | |
| **6.** cone | | | |

**Test Prep**

Fill in the ○ for the correct answer. NH means Not Here.

**7.** I am a shape that can roll and stack. What shape am I?

sphere      cylinder      cube      NH

○          ○          ○          ○

**Use with text pages 191–192.**

# Classifying and Sorting
# Solid Shapes

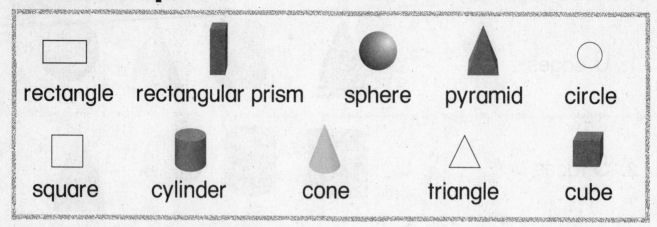

rectangle    rectangular prism    sphere    pyramid    circle

square    cylinder    cone    triangle    cube

Sort the shapes. Write the name.

**1.**    **Plane Shapes**        **2.**    **Solid Shapes**

circle
_____       _____

_____       _____

_____       _____

_____       _____

      _____

      _____

**Test Prep**

Fill in the ○ for the correct answer. NH means Not Here.

**3.** I am a solid shape with **6** faces. What am I?

            NH

○       ○       ○       ○

**Use with text pages 193–194.**

Name _____ Date _____

# Identify Faces of a Solid Shape

Look at the plane shape.
Circle the solid with a face like it.

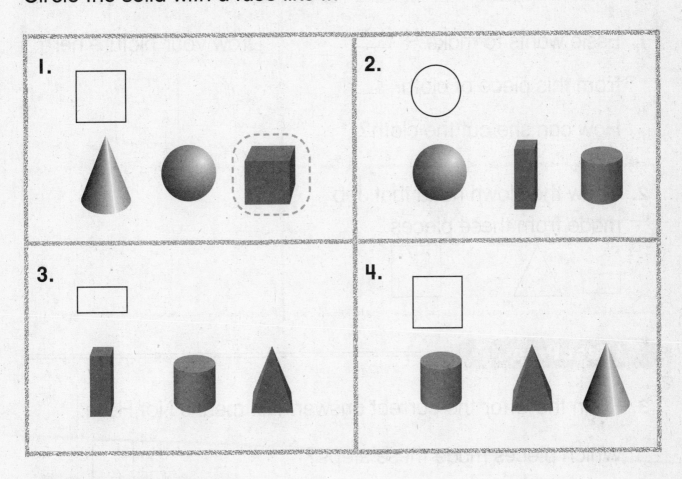

1.

2.

3.

4.

**Test Prep**

Fill in the ○ for the correct answer. NH means Not Here.

5. Which solid does NOT have a face that is a square?

NH

○          ○          ○          ○

**Use with text pages 195–196.**

Name _____ Date _____

# Problem Solving Strategy: Draw a Picture

1. Essie wants to make 4  from this piece of cloth. How can she cut the cloth?

Draw your picture here.

2. Show the clown head that Jeb made from these pieces.

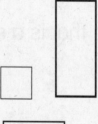

---

**Test Prep**

3. Fill in the ○ for the correct answer. NH means Not Here.

Which pieces made these steps?

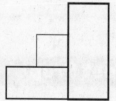

 ○

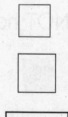 ○

○

NH ○

**Use with text pages 197–199.**

# Position Words

Follow the directions.

Draw the object.

**I.** Draw an 🌰 to the

right of 🐿️ .

**2.** Draw a ☀️ over the 🌳 .

**3.** Draw a 🍀 between the

🏠 and the ⌂ .

**4.** Draw 3 🍎 under

the 🌳 .

---

**Test Prep**

Fill in the ○ for the correct answer. NH means Not Here.

**5.** In the picture above, where is the 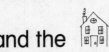 ?

left of        between the 🌳        over

the 🌳         and the 🏠          the 🌳              NH

○              ○                  ○              ○

**Use with text pages 207–208.**

# More Position Words

Circle the answer that completes the sentence.

**1.**

The 🐕 is _____ the 🏠 .

( in front of )    behind

**2.**

The 🐱 is _____ the 🌳 .

up    down

**3.**

The ⛵ is _____ the 🛶 .

far from    near

**4.**

The 🐱 is _____ the 🐕 .

far from    next to

### ✓ Test Prep

Fill in the ○ for the correct answer. NH means Not Here.

**5.** Use the word behind, near, or up to complete the sentence.

The 🪣 is _____ the 🏰 .

up      behind      near      NH
○          ○             ○          ○

**Use with text pages 209–210.**

Name _____ Date _____

# Give and Follow Directions

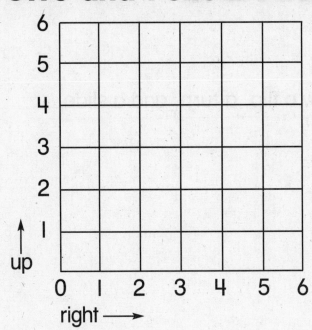

Follow the directions.

Draw an object on the grid.

| Go Right ⟶ | Go Up ↑ | Draw |
|---|---|---|
| 1. 2 spaces | 4 spaces | 🌼 |
| 2. 5 spaces | 2 spaces | ☀ |
| 3. 4 spaces | 4 spaces | 🌳 |

**Test Prep**

Fill in the ○ for the correct answer. NH means Not Here.

4. Look at the grid. Go right 2 spaces. Go up 4 spaces.

   What is next to the ?

       NH

○         ○          ○           ○

**Use with text pages 211–212.**

Name _____ Date _____

# Activity: Slides, Flips, and Turns

Use pattern blocks.

Put your block on the shape.

Move and trace your block to show a flip, a turn, and a slide.

1. Flip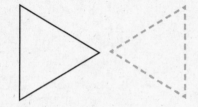

2. Turn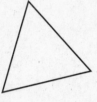

3. Slide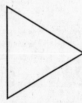

**Test Prep**

Fill in the ○ for the correct answer. NH means Not Here.

4. Look at this figure.

   Which figure below shows a flip?

|        |        |        |        |
|--------|--------|--------|--------|
| ○      | ○      | ○      | NH ○   |

**Use with text pages 215–218.**

# Patterns

Use shapes to copy the pattern.
Circle the one that comes next.

1. △ □ △ □ △ □ | (△) □

2. ○ □ ○ □ ○ □ | ○ □

3. ○ ○ ○ ○ ○ ○ | ○ ○

4. ● ○ ● ○ ● ○ | ● ○

Fill in the ○ for the correct answer. NH means Not Here.

5. Which comes next?

△        |||△        △        NH
○         ○          ○        ○

Use with text pages 219–220.

55

# Create Patterns

Use the shapes to draw a pattern.

1.

2.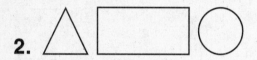

3.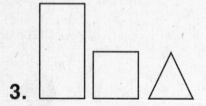

**Test Prep**

Fill in the ○ for the correct answer. NH means Not Here.

4. Which might come next?

○

○

○

NH
○

Use with text pages 221–222.

Name _____  Date _____

# Translate Patterns

Find the pattern. Draw shapes to show it another way.

1.

2.

3.

**Test Prep**

Fill in the ○ for the correct answer. NH means Not Here.

4. Which shows the pattern in another way?

○ ○△○△○△○△

○ ○○△△○○△△

○ ○△□○△□○△□

○ NH

**Use with text pages 223–224.**

Name _____ Date _____

# Symmetry

Draw a line of symmetry.

1.

2.

3.

4.

5.

6. **8**

7.

8.

9.

---

**Test Prep**

Fill in the ○ for the correct answer. NH means Not Here.

10. Which shows a line of symmetry?

            NH

○            ○            ○            ○

**Use with text pages 225–227.**

# Problem Solving:
# Find a Pattern

Solve.

1. Becky makes this pattern on a belt.
   Put an **X** on the shape that is wrong in the pattern.
   Draw the correct shape.

2. Bella makes a necklace with this pattern.
   Circle the shape that comes next.

 **Test Prep**

Fill in the ○ for the correct answer. NH means Not Here.

3. Look at the pattern.
   Which figure comes next?

    ☐                        NH

  ○             ○             ○            ○

**Use with text pages 229–231.**

Practice
9.1

# Equal Parts

1. Circle the shape that shows equal parts.

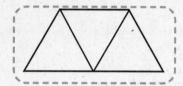  

Write the number of equal parts.

2.

_____ equal parts

3.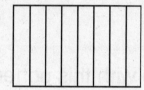

_____ equal parts

4.

_____ equal parts

5.

_____ equal parts

6.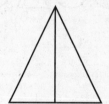

_____ equal parts

7.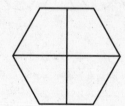

_____ equal parts

### Test Prep

Fill in the ○ for the correct answer. NH means Not Here.

8. Which shape has **3** equal parts?

NH

○             ○             ○             ○

**Use with text pages 239–240.**

Name _____ Date _____

# One Half

Color $\frac{1}{2}$.

1.

2.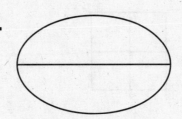

3.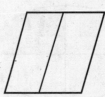

4.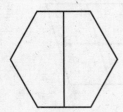

5.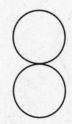

6.

Draw a line to show halves.

7.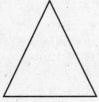

8.

9.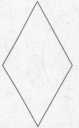

**Test Prep**

Fill in the ○ for the correct answer. NH means Not Here.

10. Debbie wants $\frac{1}{2}$ a pizza.

Which picture shows halves?

                NH

○                              ○                              ○                              ○

**Use with text pages 241–242.**

Name _____ Date _____

# One Fourth

Color $\frac{1}{4}$.

1.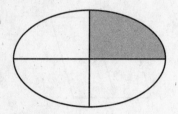

2.

3.

4.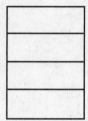

5.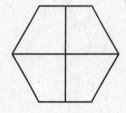

6.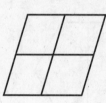

Draw lines to show fourths.

7.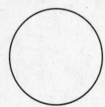

8.

9.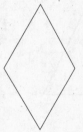

---

**Test Prep**

Fill in the ○ for the correct answer. NH means Not Here.

10. Jill wants one third of an apple. How many equal pieces will the apple be divided into?

    4    3    2    NH
    ○    ○    ○    ○

    Explain how you can tell if an apple is divided into thirds.

    _____

    _____

    _____

**Use with text pages 243–244.**

Name _____ Date _____

# Fractions of a Set

Color to show the fraction.

1. $\dfrac{1}{3}$

2. $\dfrac{1}{2}$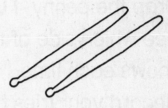

3. $\dfrac{1}{4}$

4. $\dfrac{1}{3}$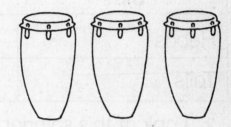

5. $\dfrac{1}{2}$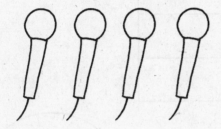

6. $\dfrac{1}{4}$

**Test Prep**

Fill in the ○ for the correct answer. NH means Not Here.

7. Which set shows $\dfrac{1}{4}$?

  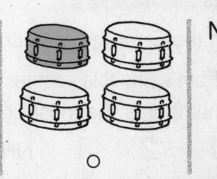 NH

○          ○          ○          ○

**Use with text pages 247–248.**

Name _____ Date _____

# Activity: Probability

1. Use a .
   Drop the penny 10 times.
   See which side of the penny
   shows each time.
   Record your tries here.

| Side | Tally |
|------|-------|
| Heads | |
| Tails | |

2. Look at this spinner. What
   letter do you predict you would
   spin most often? _____

   Check your prediction. Spin 10 times.
   Record your spins.

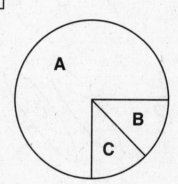

| Letter | Tally |
|--------|-------|
| A | |
| B | |
| C | |

### Test Prep

Fill in the ○ for the correct answer. NH means Not Here.

3. Pam spins this spinner. What
   number is she most likely to spin?

   1    2    3    NH
   ○    ○    ○    ○

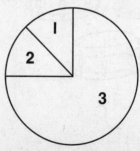

Use with text pages 249–250.

# Problem Solving:
# Use a Picture

Use the picture to solve.

1.  Emma takes a cookie without looking. Which shape is she more likely to pick?

Draw or write to explain.

_____

2.  How many more cookies have circle shapes than square shapes?

_____ more cookies have circle shapes.

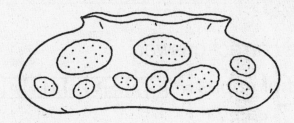

3.  Kelly takes a cracker from the bag. Is she more likely to take a large cracker or a small cracker?

_____

**Use with text pages 253–255.**

# Count Tens

Write the number of tens.
Write the number.

1. □□□□□□□□□□ □□□□□□□□□□
   □□□□□□□□□□ □□□□□□□□□□    __4__ tens
                           __40__
                           forty

2. □□□□□□□□□□ □□□□□□□□□□
   □□□□□□□□□□ □□□□□□□□□□    _____ tens
   □□□□□□□□□□
                           _____
                           fifty

3. □□□□□□□□□□ □□□□□□□□□□
   □□□□□□□□□□ □□□□□□□□□□    _____ tens
   □□□□□□□□□□ □□□□□□□□□□
                           _____
                           sixty

**Test Prep**

Fill in the ○ for the correct answer.

4. This is one set of cubes.   □□□□□□□□□□
   How many in **7** sets?

        7      10      17      70
        ○       ○       ○       ○

**Use with text pages 277–278.**

# Teen Numbers

Use Workmat 5 and ⬚.

| Show. | Regroup. Write the tens and the ones. | Write the number. |
|---|---|---|
| 1. 19 ones | _____ ten _____ ones | _____ |
| 2. 11 ones | _____ ten _____ one | _____ |
| 3. 17 ones | _____ ten _____ ones | _____ |
| 4. 12 ones | _____ ten _____ ones | _____ |
| 5. 16 ones | _____ ten _____ ones | _____ |
| 6. 18 ones | _____ ten _____ ones | _____ |
| 7. 15 ones | _____ ten _____ ones | _____ |
| 8. 13 ones | _____ ten _____ ones | _____ |
| 9. 14 ones | _____ ten _____ ones | _____ |

## Test Prep

Fill in the ○ for the correct answer. NH means Not Here.

10. What word names the missing number?

sixteen _____ eighteen

seventeen      fifteen      eleven      NH

    ○          ○          ○          ○

**Use with text pages 279–280.**

Name _____ Date _____

# Tens and Ones

Use Workmat 5 and ⌐o⌐.

| Show. | Regroup. Write the tens and the ones. | Write the number. |
|---|---|---|
| 1. 32 ones | __3__ tens __2__ ones | __32__ |
| 2. 15 ones | _____ ten _____ ones | _____ |
| 3. 40 ones | _____ tens _____ ones | _____ |
| 4. 12 ones | _____ ten _____ ones | _____ |
| 5. 29 ones | _____ tens _____ ones | _____ |
| 6. 41 ones | _____ tens _____ one | _____ |
| 7. 18 ones | _____ ten _____ ones | _____ |
| 8. 37 ones | _____ tens _____ ones | _____ |
| 9. 22 ones | _____ tens _____ ones | _____ |

**Test Prep**

Fill in the ○ for the correct answer. NH means Not Here.

10. What word name is the same as 1 ten and 5 ones?

| seventeen | fifteen | eleven | NH |
|---|---|---|---|
| ○ | ○ | ○ | ○ |

Use with text pages 281–282.

# Numbers Through 50

Use Workmat 5, ▭▭▭▭▭, and ▱.

Show and write the tens and the ones.

Write the number.

**1.**

| Workmat 5 | |
|---|---|
| Tens | Ones |

_2_ tens

_7_ ones

_27_

twenty-seven

**2.**

| Workmat 5 | |
|---|---|
| Tens | Ones |

_____ tens

_____ ones

_____

thirty-five

**3.**

| Workmat 5 | |
|---|---|
| Tens | Ones |

_____ tens

_____ ones

_____

forty-nine

**4.**

| Workmat 5 | |
|---|---|
| Tens | Ones |

_____ tens

_____ one

_____

forty-one

### Test Prep

Fill in the ○ for the correct answer. NH means Not Here.

**5.** How many in all?

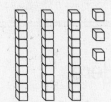

13      23      33      NH

○        ○        ○        ○

Explain your answer.

**Use with text pages 283–284.**

Name _____ Date _____

# Numbers Through 99

Write the tens and the ones. Write the number.

1.

| Tens | Ones |
|------|------|
| 5 | 3 |

___53___  fifty-three

2.

| Tens | Ones |
|------|------|
|  |  |

_____  seventy-five

3.

| Tens | Ones |
|------|------|
|  |  |

_____  eighty-seven

4.

| Tens | Ones |
|------|------|
|  |  |

_____  sixty-one

5.

| Tens | Ones |
|------|------|
|  |  |

_____  ninety-eight

6.

| Tens | Ones |
|------|------|
|  |  |

_____  fifty-seven

**Test Prep**

Fill in the ○ for the correct answer. NH means Not Here.

7. How many in all?

53      43      35      NH
○        ○        ○        ○

**Use with text pages 285–287.**

# Place Value Through 99

Write the tens in the tens place.
Write the ones in the ones place.
Write the number.

**1.**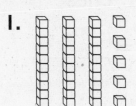

| Tens | Ones |
|------|------|
| 3    | 5    |

35

**2.**

| Tens | Ones |
|------|------|
|      |      |

_____

**3.**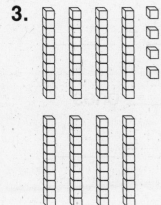

| Tens | Ones |
|------|------|
|      |      |

_____

**4.**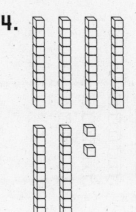

| Tens | Ones |
|------|------|
|      |      |

_____

**Test Prep**

Fill in the ○ for the correct answer.

**5.** How many tens are there in the number 95?

90        19        10        9
○          ○          ○          ○

Use with text pages 289–290.

Name _____  Date _____

# Different Ways to Show Numbers

Write the number in different ways.

1.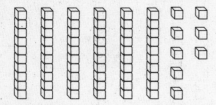

  __3__ tens __4__ ones

  __30__ + __4__ = __34__

2.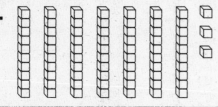

  _____ tens _____ ones

  _____ + _____ = _____

3.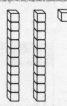

  _____ tens _____ one

  _____ + _____ = _____

4.

  _____ tens _____ ones

  _____ + _____ = _____

5.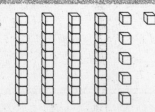

  _____ tens _____ ones

  _____ + _____ = _____

**Test Prep**

Fill in the ○ for the correct answer.

6. What is another way to write 5 tens and 6 ones?

  65        56        55        50
  ○         ○         ○         ○

**Use with text pages 291–292.**

Name _____ Date _____

# Numbers Through 100

Write how many tens and ones. Write the number.

**1.**

_____1_____ ten _____3_____ ones

_____13_____ thirteen

**2.**

_____ tens _____ ones

_____ eighty-four

**3.**

_____ tens _____ ones

_____ sixty

**4.**

_____ tens _____ ones

_____ seventy-six

**Test Prep**

Fill in the ○ for the correct answer. NH means Not Here.

**5.** What is another way to write 10 tens?

1          10          100          NH

○              ○              ○              ○

**Use with text pages 293–294.**

Name _____ Date _____

# Problem Solving:
# Act It Out With Models

Use 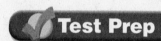 and ⬡ to solve.

Draw or write to explain.

1. Rick puts 43 action figures in cases. Each case holds 10 action figures. How many cases does Rick use?

_5_ cases

2. Ling puts 36 muffins in boxes. Each box holds 10 muffins. How many boxes does Ling need?

_____ boxes

**Test Prep**

Fill in the ○ for the correct answer.

3. Gina puts 47 books in a bookcase. 10 books fit on each shelf. How many shelves does she use?

4    5    7    10
○    ○    ○    ○

Explain your answer.

Use with text pages 295–297.

# Order Numbers

Use Workmats 7 and 8.

Write the number that comes just before or just after.

1. __72__, 73

2. 77, _____

3. _____, 81

4. 83, _____

5. _____, 71

6. _____, 80

Write the number that comes between.

7. 72, _____, 74

8. 79, _____, 81

9. 75, _____, 77

10. 77, _____, 79

11. 80, _____, 82

12. 74, _____, 76

Write the missing numbers.
Count forward or backward.

13. 42, _____, _____, 45

14. 19, _____, _____, 16

15. 62, _____, _____, 65

16. 37, _____, _____, 40

## Test Prep

Fill in the ○ for the correct answer. NH means Not Here.

17. Marisa sits in the seat between 24 and 26.
    What is her seat number?

    2      25      27      NH
    ○      ○       ○       ○

**Use with text pages 305–306.**

Name _____  Date _____

# Ordinal Numbers

Color.

1. first
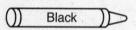
Black

2. third
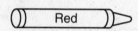
Red

3. seventh
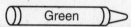
Green

4. second
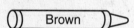
Brown

5. ninth

Yellow

6. fifth
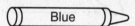
Blue

7. first
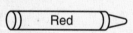
Red

8. tenth
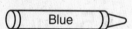
Blue

9. sixth
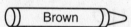
Brown

10. fourth
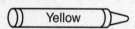
Yellow

11. eighth
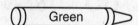
Green

12. second
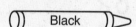
Black

## Test Prep

Fill in the ○ for the correct answer.

13. Terry is fifth in line. Avi is in front of her.
   In what place in line is Avi?

   sixth        fifth        fourth        third
    ○            ○            ○             ○

**Use with text pages 307–308.**

Name _____ Date _____

# Use Ten to Estimate

Circle one group of ten. Estimate about how many in all.
Then count.

1.

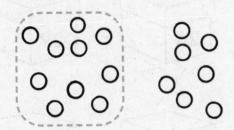

| Estimate |
|:---:|
| 20 |
| Count |
| 17 |

2.

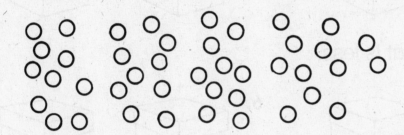

| Estimate |
|:---:|
| |
| Count |
| |

3.

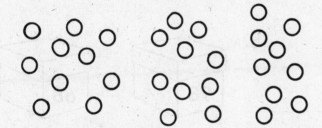

| Estimate |
|:---:|
| |
| Count |
| |

 **Test Prep**

Fill in the ○ for the correct answer.
NH means Not Here.

4. Jan dropped her crayons. About
   how many crayons does she have?

about 10       about 20       about 30       NH
   ○               ○               ○          ○

**Use with text pages 309–311.**

Name _____ Date _____

# Greater Than, Less Than

Circle the number that is greater.

1.  42 33

2.  26 29

3.  90 80

4.  54 55

Circle the number that is less.

5.  51 15

6.  39 40

7.  70 77

8.  98 68

**Test Prep**

Fill in the ○ for the correct answer. NH means Not Here.

9. Lindsey has 35 markers.

Nick has fewer markers than Lindsey.

How many markers does Nick have?

53    40    30    NH
○      ○      ○     ○

Use with text pages 313–314.

# Use Symbols to Compare Numbers

Compare. Circle >, <, or =.

1.  (>) < =

2.  > < =

3.  > < =

4.  > < =

5.  > < =

6.  > < =

7.  > < =

8.  > < =

**Test Prep**

Fill in the ○ for the correct answer.

9. Maria's basket has 46 apples.
   The number in Mike's basket is
   equal to the number in Maria's basket.
   How many apples are in Mike's basket?

   40      46      50      64
   ○        ○        ○        ○

Use with text pages 315–316.

# Problem Solving:
# Reasonable Answers

Estimate. Circle the answer that makes sense.

**1.** Kate goes to see a movie.

About how long is the movie?

about **2** hours

about **10** hours

**2.** First graders take a bus trip.

About how many children sit in
the bus?

about **3** children

about **30** children

**3.** Ellen baby-sits her younger brother.

About how old is her brother?

about **6** years old

about **16** years old

**4.** Ben bakes some muffins.

About how many cups of flour
does he use?

about **2** cups

about **22** cups

**5.** Eli reads a book before going
to bed. He starts after taking
his bath. About how many
hours does Eli read?

about **11** hours

about **1** hour

**Use with text pages 317–318.**

# Count by Twos

Write the missing numbers.
Skip count by 2s.

| 1 | 2 | 3 | 4 | 5 | 6 | 7 | 8 | 9 | 10 |
|---|---|---|---|---|---|---|---|---|----|
| 11 | 12 | 13 | 14 | 15 | 16 | 17 | 18 | 19 | 20 |
| 21 | 22 | 23 | 24 | 25 | 26 | 27 | 28 | 29 | 30 |
| 31 | 32 | 33 | 34 | 35 | 36 | 37 | 38 | 39 | 40 |
| 41 | 42 | 43 | 44 | 45 | 46 | 47 | 48 | 49 | 50 |
| 51 | 52 | 53 | 54 | 55 | 56 | 57 | 58 | 59 | 60 |
| 61 | 62 | 63 | 64 | 65 | 66 | 67 | 68 | 69 | 70 |
| 71 | 72 | 73 | 74 | 75 | 76 | 77 | 78 | 79 | 80 |
| 81 | 82 | 83 | 84 | 85 | 86 | 87 | 88 | 89 | 90 |
| 91 | 92 | 93 | 94 | 95 | 96 | 97 | 98 | 99 | 100 |

1. 18, _20_, _22_, 24

2. 32, 34, _____, _____, 40

3. 64, _____, _____, 70

4. 46, 48, _____, _____

5. 54, _____, _____, 60

6. 86, _____, _____, _____, _____, _____

7. 54, _____, _____, 60, _____, _____

8. 92, _____, _____, _____, _____

9. Skip count by 2s from 22 to 50.

Use ▭▷ to color the numbers you say.

**Test Prep**

Fill in the ○ for the correct answer.

10. If you count by 2s from 20 to 50,
which number would you say?

23     44     52     66
○        ○        ○        ○

Use with text pages 325–326.

Name _____  Date _____

# Count by Fives

Write the missing numbers.
Skip count by 5s.

| 1 | 2 | 3 | 4 | 5 | 6 | 7 | 8 | 9 | 10 |
|---|---|---|---|---|---|---|---|---|---|
| 11 | 12 | 13 | 14 | 15 | 16 | 17 | 18 | 19 | 20 |
| 21 | 22 | 23 | 24 | 25 | 26 | 27 | 28 | 29 | 30 |
| 31 | 32 | 33 | 34 | 35 | 36 | 37 | 38 | 39 | 40 |
| 41 | 42 | 43 | 44 | 45 | 46 | 47 | 48 | 49 | 50 |
| 51 | 52 | 53 | 54 | 55 | 56 | 57 | 58 | 59 | 60 |
| 61 | 62 | 63 | 64 | 65 | 66 | 67 | 68 | 69 | 70 |
| 71 | 72 | 73 | 74 | 75 | 76 | 77 | 78 | 79 | 80 |
| 81 | 82 | 83 | 84 | 85 | 86 | 87 | 88 | 89 | 90 |
| 91 | 92 | 93 | 94 | 95 | 96 | 97 | 98 | 99 | 100 |

1. 25, __30__, __35__, __40__

2. 30, 35, _____, _____, 50

3. 55, _____, _____, 70

4. 70, _____, _____, 85

5. 60, _____, _____, _____

6. 80, _____, _____, _____, _____

Count back by 5s.

7. 65, 60, _____, _____, _____, 40

8. 30, _____, _____, _____, _____, _____, 0

9. Skip count by 5s from 50 to 100.

Use 🖍 to color the numbers you say.

**✓ Test Prep**

Fill in the ○ for the correct answer. NH means Not Here.

10. If you count by 5s from 20 to 80,
    which number would you say?

    5        15       100      NH
    ○         ○         ○        ○

Use with text pages 327–328.

Name _____ Date _____

# More Than, Less Than

Write the number that is 1 more.

1. 39 __40__    2. 77 _____

3. 53 _____    4. 80 _____

Write the number that is 1 less.

5. _____ 30    6. _____ 58

7. _____ 86    8. _____ 100

Write the number that is 10 more.

| 1 | 2 | 3 | 4 | 5 | 6 | 7 | 8 | 9 | 10 |
|---|---|---|---|---|---|---|---|---|---|
| 11 | 12 | 13 | 14 | 15 | 16 | 17 | 18 | 19 | 20 |
| 21 | 22 | 23 | 24 | 25 | 26 | 27 | 28 | 29 | 30 |
| 31 | 32 | 33 | 34 | 35 | 36 | 37 | 38 | 39 | 40 |
| 41 | 42 | 43 | 44 | 45 | 46 | 47 | 48 | 49 | 50 |
| 51 | 52 | 53 | 54 | 55 | 56 | 57 | 58 | 59 | 60 |
| 61 | 62 | 63 | 64 | 65 | 66 | 67 | 68 | 69 | 70 |
| 71 | 72 | 73 | 74 | 75 | 76 | 77 | 78 | 79 | 80 |
| 81 | 82 | 83 | 84 | 85 | 86 | 87 | 88 | 89 | 90 |
| 91 | 92 | 93 | 94 | 95 | 96 | 97 | 98 | 99 | 100 |

9. 21    10. 45    11. 57    12. 60    13. 83

_____   _____   _____   _____   _____

Write the number that is 10 less.

14. _____    15. _____    16. _____    17. _____    18. _____

25         30         53         71         89

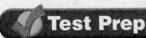 **Test Prep**

Fill in the ○ for the correct answer.

19. Mary has 23 dolls.

Susan has 10 more than Mary.

How many dolls does Susan have?

43        33        23        13
○         ○         ○         ○

Use with text pages 329–330.

# Even and Odd Numbers

Circle even or odd.

**1.** 13

odd    even

**2.** 16

odd    even

**3.** 9

odd    even

**4.** 6

odd    even

**5.** 10

odd    even

**6.** 19

odd    even

**7.** Color the even numbers (Yellow).

Color the odd numbers (Purple).

| 51 | 52 | 53 | 54 | 55 | 56 | 57 | 58 | 59 | 60 |
|----|----|----|----|----|----|----|----|----|----|
| 61 | 62 | 63 | 64 | 65 | 66 | 67 | 68 | 69 | 70 |
| 71 | 72 | 73 | 74 | 75 | 76 | 77 | 78 | 79 | 80 |

**Test Prep**

Fill in the ○ for the correct answer.  NH means Not Here.

**8.** Which number is an odd number?

36    53    88    NH

○     ○     ○     ○

**Use with text pages 333–334.**

# Problem Solving:
# Find a Pattern

Find the pattern. Solve.

1. Jack walks his dog 2 times each day. How many times does he walk the dog in 5 days?

| Day 1 | Day 2 | Day 3 | Day 4 | Day 5 |
|-------|-------|-------|-------|-------|
| 2 |  |  |  |  |
| He walks the dog _____ times. |  |  |  |  |

2. Susie reads 5 books each week. How many books does she read in 5 weeks?

| Week 1 | Week 2 | Week 3 | Week 4 | Week 5 |
|--------|--------|--------|--------|--------|
|  |  |  |  |  |
| She reads _____ books. |  |  |  |  |

**Test Prep**

Fill in the ○ for the correct answer.

3. Tammy reads 10 pages of her book each day. How many pages will she read in 6 days?

60      50      40      10
○        ○        ○        ○

Explain how you found your answer.

_____

_____

**Use with text pages 335–337.**

# Order Events

Write 1, 2, and 3 to show the correct order.

## Test Prep

Fill in the ○ for the correct answer. NH means Not Here.

4. Jane is sending a postcard to a friend.
   What is the <u>last</u> thing she will do?

| Write the postcard. | Put the postcard in the mailbox. | Put a stamp on the postcard. | NH |
|---|---|---|---|
| ○ | ○ | ○ | ○ |

**Use with text pages 359–360.**

# Activity: Estimate a Minute

Circle activities you know take about 1 minute.
Draw an X on the activity if it takes more than 1 minute.

1.

2.

3.

4.

**Test Prep**

Fill in the ○ under the correct answer. NH means Not Here.

5. Which of these activities takes more than 1 minute?

    NH

○          ○          ○          ○

**Use with text pages 361–362.**

Name _____  Date _____

# Hour

Read the clock. Write the time two ways.

**1.**

$4:00$

____ o'clock

**2.**

____ o'clock

**3.**

____ o'clock

**4.**

____ o'clock

**5.**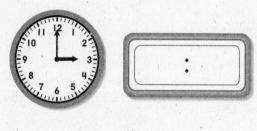

____ o'clock

**6.**

____ o'clock

**Test Prep**

Fill in the ○ for the correct answer. NH means Not Here.

**7.** What time is it on the clock?

12:00   8:00   2:00   NH

○        ○        ○        ○

**Use with text pages 363–364.**

# Half-Hour

Say and write the time.

**1.**

_____10_____ o'clock

**2.**

half past _____

**3.**

half past _____

**4.**

_____ o'clock

**Test Prep**

Fill in the ○ for the correct answer. NH means Not Here.

**5.** Abby begins reading at **5:30**.
Which clock shows the time?

         NH

○            ○            ○            ○

**Use with text pages 365–367.**

# Elapsed Time

Use a clock.

Show when the activity starts or ends.

| Start | How long? | End |
|---|---|---|

**1.**

1 hour reading

**2.**

`: `

1 hour cooking

**6 : 00**

**3.**

2 hours driving

---

**Test Prep**

Fill in the ○ for the correct answer. NH means Not Here.

**4.** The movie starts at **5:00**. It lasts **2** hours.

What time is it over?

○    ○    ○    ○ NH

Use with text pages 369–371.

# Practice Telling Time

Show the time on the clock.

**1.** I get up at **7** o'clock.

**2.** I eat breakfast at half past **7**.

 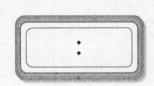

**3.** I help mom at half past **8**.

 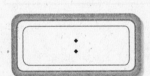

**4.** I walk the dog at **11** o'clock.

**Test Prep**

Fill in the ○ for the correct answer. NH means Not Here.

**5.** Phillip gets home at **4** o'clock.
Which clock shows the time?

      NH

○             ○             ○             ○

**Use with text pages 373–374.**

# Days and Weeks

Fill in the calendar for this month.

| Saturday | Monday | Tuesday | Wednesday | Thursday | Friday | Saturday |
|----------|--------|---------|-----------|----------|--------|----------|
|          |        |         |           |          |        |          |
|          |        |         |           |          |        |          |
|          |        |         |           |          |        |          |
|          |        |         |           |          |        |          |
|          |        |         |           |          |        |          |

1. Color today ◯▭ Red ▭▷.

2. What is the date of the second Monday in this month? _____

3. What day of the week is the last day in this month? _____

### Test Prep

Fill in the ○ for the correct answer. NH means Not Here.

4. Andrew's birthday is on June 5.
   His party is two days later.
   What is the date of his party?

   June 3        June 6        June 7        NH

   ○            ○            ○            ○

**Use with text pages 375–376.**

Name _____    Date _____

# Months

Use the calendars to find the answer.

| | August | | | | | | |
|---|---|---|---|---|---|---|---|
| S | M | T | W | T | F | S |
| | | 1 | 2 | 3 | 4 | 5 |
| 6 | 7 | 8 | 9 | 10 | 11 | 12 |
| 13 | 14 | 15 | 16 | 17 | 18 | 19 |
| 20 | 21 | 22 | 23 | 24 | 25 | 26 |
| 27 | 28 | 29 | 30 | 31 | | |

| | September | | | | | | |
|---|---|---|---|---|---|---|---|
| S | M | T | W | T | F | S |
| | | | | | 1 | 2 |
| 3 | 4 | 5 | 6 | 7 | 8 | 9 |
| 10 | 11 | 12 | 13 | 14 | 15 | 16 |
| 17 | 18 | 19 | 20 | 21 | 22 | 23 |
| 24 | 25 | 26 | 27 | 28 | 29 | 30 |

| | October | | | | | | |
|---|---|---|---|---|---|---|---|
| S | M | T | W | T | F | S |
| 1 | 2 | 3 | 4 | 5 | 6 | 7 |
| 8 | 9 | 10 | 11 | 12 | 13 | 14 |
| 15 | 16 | 17 | 18 | 19 | 20 | 21 |
| 22 | 23 | 24 | 25 | 26 | 27 | 28 |
| 29 | 30 | 31 | | | | |

1. Which month has 5 Fridays? __September__

2. School begins on September 6. Color it green.

3. Use ⟨ Red ⟩. Color all Tuesdays in October.

4. Use ⟨ Blue ⟩. Color August 10.

## Test Prep

Fill in the ○ for the correct answer. NH means Not Here.

5. Lily goes on a trip on Friday.
   She comes back 2 days later.
   On which day does she come back?

   Sunday          Saturday          Thursday          NH

   ○               ○                 ○                 ○

Use with text pages 377–378.

Name _____ Date _____

# Problem Solving: Use a Table

Use the table to solve the problem.

## Monday Schedule

| Activity | Time |
|----------|------|
| Reading | 9:00 |
| Math | 11:00 |
| Lunch | 12:00 |
| Science | 1:00 |
| Art | 2:00 |
| Dismissal | 3:00 |

Draw or write
to explain.

1. Ms. Roper gets to school at **8:00**. How much time does she have before Reading?

_____1 hour_____

2. What activity starts **2** hours before Science?

_____

3. What activity starts **2** hours after lunch starts?

_____

4. How many hours are there between Reading and Lunch?

_____

**Use with text pages 379–381.**

# Value of Coins

Find the value of the coins.

1.     

___1___¢    ___2___¢    ___3___¢    ___4___¢    ___5___¢    | 5 | ¢

2.

_____¢    _____¢    _____¢    _____¢    _____¢    |      | ¢

3.

_____¢  _____¢  _____¢  _____¢  _____¢  _____¢    |      | ¢

**Test Prep**

Fill in the ○ for the correct answer. NH means Not Here.

4. What is the value of the coins?

50¢         40¢         80¢         NH
○           ○           ○           ○

**Use with text pages 389–390.**

Name _____ Date _____

# Nickels and Pennies

Find the value of the coins.

1.

   <u>5</u> ¢  <u>10</u> ¢  <u>11</u> ¢  <u>12</u> ¢  <u>13</u> ¢  <u>14</u> ¢  | 14 | ¢

2.

   ____ ¢  ____ ¢  ____ ¢  ____ ¢  ____ ¢  ____ ¢  |  | ¢

3.

   ____ ¢  ____ ¢  ____ ¢  ____ ¢  ____ ¢  ____ ¢  |  | ¢

**Test Prep**

Fill in the ○ for the correct answer. NH means Not Here.

4. What is the value of the coins?

   23¢         33¢         28¢         NH
    ○           ○           ○           ○

**Use with text pages 391–392.**

Name _____ Date _____

# Dimes and Pennies

Circle the group of coins that matches the price.

**1.**  32¢

**2.** 40¢

**3.** 41¢

**4.** 41¢

---

## Test Prep

Fill in the ○ for the correct answer. NH means Not Here.

**5.** What is the value of the coins?

23¢     43¢     18¢     NH
○         ○         ○         ○

**Use with text pages 393–394.**

Name _____   Date _____

# Count Coins

Use coins.

Find the value of the coins.

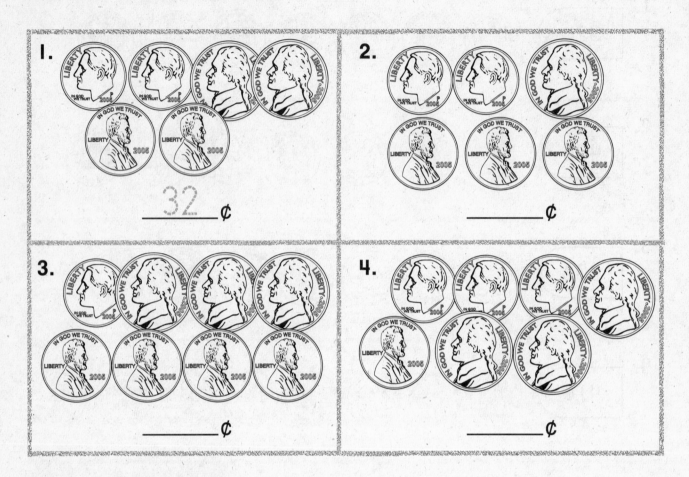

1. _____ 32 ¢

2. _____ ¢

3. _____ ¢

4. _____ ¢

---

**Test Prep**

Fill in the ○ for the correct answer. NH means Not Here.

5. What is the value of the coins?

33¢    58¢    41¢    NH

○        ○        ○        ○

**Use with text pages 395–396.**

# Quarters

Use coins.

Circle the coins that match the price.

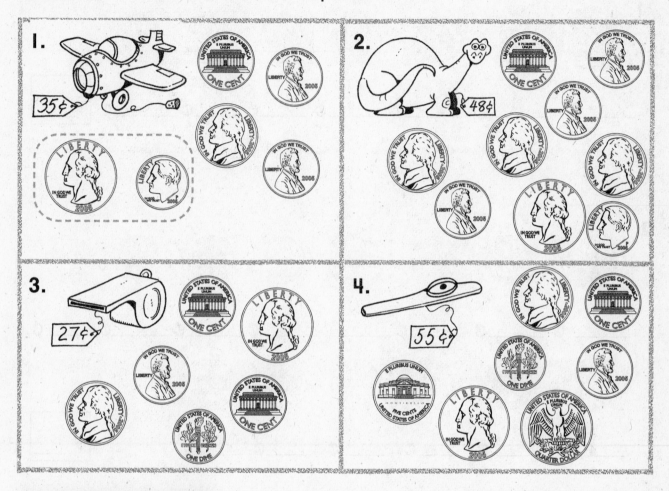

1. 35¢

2. 48¢

3. 27¢

4. 55¢

### Test Prep

Fill in the ○ for the correct answer. NH means Not Here.

5. What price matches the coins?

46¢     41¢     36¢     NH

○          ○          ○          ○

**Use with text pages 399–401.**

Name _____ Date _____

# Dollar

Find the value of the coins.

1.

25 ¢   50 ¢   60 ¢   70 ¢   80 ¢   90 ¢   100 ¢   $ 1

2.

_____ ¢ _____ ¢ _____ ¢ _____ ¢ _____ ¢ _____ ¢ _____ ¢ _____ ¢

_____ ¢ _____ ¢ _____ ¢ _____ ¢ _____ ¢ _____ ¢   $_____

## Test Prep

Fill in the ○ for the correct answer. NH means Not Here.

3. What price matches the coins?

85¢   95¢   $1   NH

○    ○    ○    ○

**Use with text pages 403–404.**

# Problem Solving: Use a Picture

Use coins to solve.

| | |
|---|---|
| **1.** Rafael wants to buy the lion. He has 15¢. What other coins might he use to buy the lion? | |
| **2.** Eric wants to buy the pencil case. He has 2 dimes and a nickel. How many more dimes does he need? | |

**Test Prep**

Fill in the ○ for the correct answer. NH means Not Here.

**3.** Leo has a quarter and 3 nickels. How much more does he need to buy juice for 50¢?

5¢    10¢    25¢    NH
○     ○     ○     ○

Use with text pages 405–407.

Name _____ Date _____

# Count On to Add

Use the number line.
Write the sum.

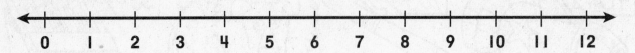

1. $5 + 3 =$ ___8___  2. $9 + 2 =$ ___  3. $8 + 1 =$ ___

4. $4 + 1 =$ ___  5. $7 + 3 =$ ___  6. $3 + 8 =$ ___

7. $6 + 2 =$ ___  8. $9 + 1 =$ ___  9. $7 + 1 =$ ___

10. $8 + 2 =$ ___  11. $5 + 2 =$ ___  12. $9 + 3 =$ ___

13. $2 + 7 =$ ___  14. $3 + 4 =$ ___  15. $3 + 6 =$ ___

**Test Prep**

Fill in the ○ for the correct answer. NH means Not Here.

16. Shawn had 7 pennies. He
found 3 more pennies.
How many pennies did he
have in all?

8    10    12    NH
○     ○      ○     ○

| Explain your answer. |
| --- |
|  |
|  |
|  |
|  |

**Use with text pages 429–430.**

Name _____ Date _____

# Sums of 10

Use Workmat 1 and ◯ to make 10.
Draw counters to fill the ten frame.
Complete the addition sentence.

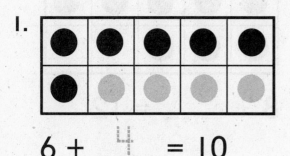

1.

$6 + \underline{4} = 10$

2.

$5 + \underline{\phantom{0}} = 10$

Write the sum.

3. $3 + 7 = \underline{\phantom{0}}$   4. $0 + 9 = \underline{\phantom{0}}$   5. $6 + 2 = \underline{\phantom{0}}$

6. $3 + 3 = \underline{\phantom{0}}$   7. $8 + 1 = \underline{\phantom{0}}$   8. $4 + 5 = \underline{\phantom{0}}$

## Test Prep

Fill in the ○ for the correct answer. NH means Not Here.

9. There are 10 spaces on a game board. Ben has moved 7 spaces. How many spaces does he still have to move?

| Explain your answer. |
| --- |
|  |

7     5     3     NH
○     ○     ○     ○

Use with text pages 431–432.

Name _____ Date _____

# Making 10 to Add

Use Workmat 1 and ◯ to help you find the sum.
Write the sum.

1.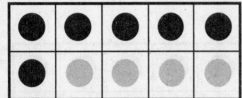

6 + __5__ = 11

2. 

8 + ___ = 12

Write the sum.

3. 7 + 4 = ___    4. 6 + 6 = ___    5. 3 + 8 = ___

6. 9 + 3 = ___    7. 4 + 7 = ___    8. 2 + 9 = ___

9.      6      5     10.    8      2     11.    7      5
      + 5    + 6          + 2    + 8          + 5    + 7
      ___    ___          ___    ___          ___    ___

**Test Prep**

Fill in the ○ for the correct answer. NH means Not Here.

12. Adam has 5 books about sports. He has 6 books about animals. How many books does he have in all?

    8      9      10      NH
    ○      ○      ○       ○

| Explain your answer. |
| --- |
|  |

**Use with text pages 433–434.**

# Order Property

Write the sum.

1.
$$7 \quad\quad 5$$
$$+5 \quad +7$$
$$12 \quad\quad 12$$

2.
$$6 \quad\quad 2$$
$$+2 \quad +6$$

3.
$$4 \quad\quad 6$$
$$+6 \quad +4$$

4.
$$8 \quad\quad 3$$
$$+3 \quad +8$$

5.
$$3 \quad\quad 4$$
$$+4 \quad +3$$

6.
$$7 \quad\quad 3$$
$$+3 \quad +7$$

7.
$$3 \quad\quad 5$$
$$+5 \quad +3$$

8.
$$8 \quad\quad 4$$
$$+4 \quad +8$$

9.
$$6 \quad\quad 5$$
$$+5 \quad +6$$

10. $4 + 3 =$ ____   11. $1 + 8 =$ ____   12. $9 + 0 =$ ____

$3 + 4 =$ ____   $8 + 1 =$ ____   $0 + 9 =$ ____

**Test Prep**

Fill in the ○ for the correct answer. NH means Not Here.

13. Brendan needs 12 nails for a
project. He has 6 nails. How
many more nails does he need?

6     5     4     NH
○     ○     ○     ○

**Use with text pages 435–436.**

# Addition Facts Practice

Use any strategy.
Find the sum.

1. $6 + 6 = \underline{12}$    2. $3 + 7 = \underline{\phantom{00}}$    3. $2 + 5 = \underline{\phantom{00}}$

4. $1 + 9 = \underline{\phantom{00}}$    5. $4 + 6 = \underline{\phantom{00}}$    6. $5 + 3 = \underline{\phantom{00}}$

7. $\begin{array}{r} 1 \\ + 5 \\ \hline \end{array}$    8. $\begin{array}{r} 3 \\ + 2 \\ \hline \end{array}$    9. $\begin{array}{r} 7 \\ + 2 \\ \hline \end{array}$    10. $\begin{array}{r} 8 \\ + 4 \\ \hline \end{array}$    11. $\begin{array}{r} 9 \\ + 3 \\ \hline \end{array}$    12. $\begin{array}{r} 8 \\ + 2 \\ \hline \end{array}$

13. $\begin{array}{r} 2 \\ + 4 \\ \hline \end{array}$    14. $\begin{array}{r} 5 \\ + 6 \\ \hline \end{array}$    15. $\begin{array}{r} 7 \\ + 3 \\ \hline \end{array}$    16. $\begin{array}{r} 4 \\ + 5 \\ \hline \end{array}$    17. $\begin{array}{r} 5 \\ + 5 \\ \hline \end{array}$    18. $\begin{array}{r} 6 \\ + 3 \\ \hline \end{array}$

## Test Prep

Fill in the ○ for the correct answer. NH means Not Here.

19. Pat has 5 pencils. Doug
    has twice as many pencils.
    How many pencils does
    Doug have?

    1        10        8        NH
    ○         ○         ○         ○

Use with text pages 439–442.

# Add Three Numbers

Write the sum.

1.
$\begin{array}{r} 1 \\ 3 \\ +4 \\ \hline 8 \end{array}$

2.
$\begin{array}{r} 3 \\ 5 \\ +4 \\ \hline \end{array}$

3.
$\begin{array}{r} 7 \\ 0 \\ +4 \\ \hline \end{array}$

4.
$\begin{array}{r} 6 \\ 1 \\ +4 \\ \hline \end{array}$

5.
$\begin{array}{r} 5 \\ 2 \\ +3 \\ \hline \end{array}$

6.
$\begin{array}{r} 4 \\ 1 \\ +5 \\ \hline \end{array}$

7.
$\begin{array}{r} 2 \\ 4 \\ +4 \\ \hline \end{array}$

8.
$\begin{array}{r} 3 \\ 5 \\ +1 \\ \hline \end{array}$

9.
$\begin{array}{r} 7 \\ 1 \\ +3 \\ \hline \end{array}$

10.
$\begin{array}{r} 2 \\ 9 \\ +0 \\ \hline \end{array}$

11.
$\begin{array}{r} 3 \\ 3 \\ +5 \\ \hline \end{array}$

12.
$\begin{array}{r} 6 \\ 2 \\ +1 \\ \hline \end{array}$

13. $7 + 2 + 2 =$ _____

14. $2 + 7 + 1 =$ _____

15. $2 + 3 + 1 =$ _____

16. $4 + 2 + 1 =$ _____

## Test Prep

Fill in the ○ for the correct answer. NH means Not Here.

17. Hans has 5 stamps. He buys 2 more stamps. His mother gives him 4 more stamps. How many stamps does he have now?

9     11     7     NH
○      ○      ○      ○

Explain your answer.

**Use with text pages 443–444.**

# Missing Addends

Use cubes.
Find the missing addend.

1. ▢▢▢▢▢▢▢  $\boxed{3} + 4 = 7$

2. ▢▢▢▢▢▢▢▢  $\boxed{\phantom{0}} + 6 = 8$

3. $5 + \boxed{\phantom{0}} = 8$   4. $2 + \boxed{\phantom{0}} = 10$   5. $3 + \boxed{\phantom{0}} = 11$

6.  $\begin{array}{r} 1 \\ + \boxed{\phantom{0}} \\ \hline 8 \end{array}$

7.  $\begin{array}{r} 4 \\ + \boxed{\phantom{0}} \\ \hline 6 \end{array}$

8.  $\begin{array}{r} \boxed{\phantom{0}} \\ + 3 \\ \hline 10 \end{array}$

9.  $\begin{array}{r} 6 \\ + \boxed{\phantom{0}} \\ \hline 9 \end{array}$

10.  $\begin{array}{r} \boxed{\phantom{0}} \\ + 2 \\ \hline 11 \end{array}$

11.  $\begin{array}{r} \boxed{\phantom{0}} \\ + 4 \\ \hline 7 \end{array}$

12.  $\begin{array}{r} \boxed{\phantom{0}} \\ + 6 \\ \hline 12 \end{array}$

13.  $\begin{array}{r} \boxed{\phantom{0}} \\ + 3 \\ \hline 5 \end{array}$

14.  $\begin{array}{r} \boxed{\phantom{0}} \\ + 5 \\ \hline 10 \end{array}$

15.  $\begin{array}{r} 2 \\ + \boxed{\phantom{0}} \\ \hline 7 \end{array}$

## Test Prep

Fill in the ○ for the correct answer. NH means Not Here.

16. Ethan has 10 model cars. 4 cars are red. How many cars are __not__ red?

   4      6      14      NH
   ○      ○      ○      ○

| Explain your answer. |
| --- |
|  |

Use with text pages 445–446.

Name _____ Date _____

# Problem Solving: Make a Table
Complete the table. Solve.

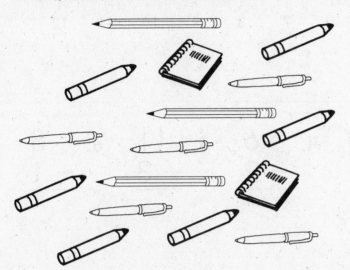

| | |
|---|---|
| Pens | |
| Pencils | 3 |
| Notebooks | |
| Markers | |

Draw or write to explain.

1. How many pencils and pens are there?

   _____ pencils and pens

2. How many more markers than notebooks are there?

   _____ markers

3. If 3 markers are added, how many markers are there?

   _____ markers

**Use with text pages 447–449.**

# Count Back to Subtract

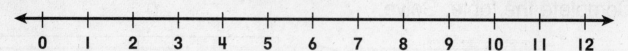

Use the number line.
Subtract.

1.  9
   – 1
    8

2.  7
   – 2

3.  10
   – 3

4.  6
   – 2

5.  11
   – 3

6.  8
   – 1

7.  5
   – 2

8.  11
   – 2

9.  9
   – 3

10. 10
   – 2

11. 9
   – 2

12. 10
   – 1

13. 8 – 3 = _____  14. 7 – 1 = _____  15. 11 – 1 = _____

## Test Prep

Fill in the ○ for the correct answer. NH means Not Here.

16. Subtract.
    12
   –  2

Explain your answer.

9    10    11    NH
○    ○    ○    ○

**Use with text pages 457–458.**

# Parts and Wholes

Write the difference.

| Whole |  |
|--------|--------|
| 11 |  |
| **Part** | **Part** |
| 9 | ? |

| Whole |  |
|--------|--------|
| 12 |  |
| **Part** | **Part** |
| 5 | ? |

| Whole |  |
|--------|--------|
| 10 |  |
| **Part** | **Part** |
| 2 | ? |

1. $11 - 9 = \underline{2}$

    $11 - 2 = \underline{9}$

2. $12 - 5 = \underline{\phantom{0}}$

    $12 - 7 = \underline{\phantom{0}}$

3. $10 - 2 = \underline{\phantom{0}}$

    $10 - 8 = \underline{\phantom{0}}$

4.
$$\begin{array}{r} 12 \\ -\ 3 \\ \hline \end{array} \quad \begin{array}{r} 12 \\ -\ 9 \\ \hline \end{array}$$

5.
$$\begin{array}{r} 10 \\ -\ 7 \\ \hline \end{array} \quad \begin{array}{r} 10 \\ -\ 3 \\ \hline \end{array}$$

6.
$$\begin{array}{r} 11 \\ -\ 7 \\ \hline \end{array} \quad \begin{array}{r} 11 \\ -\ 4 \\ \hline \end{array}$$

7.
$$\begin{array}{r} 9 \\ -\ 3 \\ \hline \end{array} \quad \begin{array}{r} 9 \\ -\ 6 \\ \hline \end{array}$$

8.
$$\begin{array}{r} 12 \\ -\ 8 \\ \hline \end{array} \quad \begin{array}{r} 12 \\ -\ 4 \\ \hline \end{array}$$

9.
$$\begin{array}{r} 11 \\ -\ 3 \\ \hline \end{array} \quad \begin{array}{r} 11 \\ -\ 8 \\ \hline \end{array}$$

## ✓ Test Prep

Fill in the ○ for the correct answer. NH means Not Here.

**10.** Subtract.

$$10 - 7$$

| 1 | 2 | 3 | NH |
|---|---|---|----|
| ○ | ○ | ○ | ○ |

Explain your answer.

**Use with text pages 459–460.**

# Relate Addition and Subtraction

Use related facts to add and subtract.

1.  $\begin{array}{r} 7 \\ +4 \\ \hline \end{array}$   $\begin{array}{r} 11 \\ -4 \\ \hline \end{array}$
2.  $\begin{array}{r} 6 \\ +3 \\ \hline \end{array}$   $\begin{array}{r} 9 \\ -3 \\ \hline \end{array}$
3.  $\begin{array}{r} 9 \\ +3 \\ \hline \end{array}$   $\begin{array}{r} 12 \\ -3 \\ \hline \end{array}$

4.  $\begin{array}{r} 6 \\ +6 \\ \hline \end{array}$   $\begin{array}{r} 12 \\ -6 \\ \hline \end{array}$
5.  $\begin{array}{r} 7 \\ +5 \\ \hline \end{array}$   $\begin{array}{r} 12 \\ -5 \\ \hline \end{array}$
6.  $\begin{array}{r} 6 \\ +4 \\ \hline \end{array}$   $\begin{array}{r} 10 \\ -4 \\ \hline \end{array}$

7.  $\begin{array}{r} 5 \\ +4 \\ \hline \end{array}$   $\begin{array}{r} 9 \\ -4 \\ \hline \end{array}$
8.  $\begin{array}{r} 2 \\ +9 \\ \hline \end{array}$   $\begin{array}{r} 11 \\ -9 \\ \hline \end{array}$
9.  $\begin{array}{r} 7 \\ +2 \\ \hline \end{array}$   $\begin{array}{r} 9 \\ -2 \\ \hline \end{array}$

10. $\begin{array}{r} 7 \\ +3 \\ \hline \end{array}$   $\begin{array}{r} 10 \\ -3 \\ \hline \end{array}$
11. $\begin{array}{r} 2 \\ +8 \\ \hline \end{array}$   $\begin{array}{r} 10 \\ -8 \\ \hline \end{array}$
12. $\begin{array}{r} 8 \\ +4 \\ \hline \end{array}$   $\begin{array}{r} 12 \\ -4 \\ \hline \end{array}$

## Test Prep

Fill in the ○ for the correct answer. NH means Not Here.

13. Find the related subtraction sentence.

$$7 + 5 = 12$$

$12 - 6 = 6$     $12 - 5 = 7$     $12 - 4 = 8$     NH

   ○         ○         ○         ○

**Use with text pages 461–462.**

Name _____ Date _____

# Subtraction Facts Practice

Use any strategy.

Find the difference.

1. $12 - 4 =$ __8__    2. $10 - 5 =$ ___    3. $9 - 6 =$ ___

4. $7 - 3 =$ ___    5. $11 - 8 =$ ___    6. $5 - 4 =$ ___

| 7. $\begin{array}{r} 6 \\ -3 \\ \hline \end{array}$ | 8. $\begin{array}{r} 9 \\ -2 \\ \hline \end{array}$ | 9. $\begin{array}{r} 12 \\ -8 \\ \hline \end{array}$ | 10. $\begin{array}{r} 7 \\ -1 \\ \hline \end{array}$ | 11. $\begin{array}{r} 11 \\ -5 \\ \hline \end{array}$ | 12. $\begin{array}{r} 2 \\ -2 \\ \hline \end{array}$ |
|---|---|---|---|---|---|
| 13. $\begin{array}{r} 10 \\ -7 \\ \hline \end{array}$ | 14. $\begin{array}{r} 12 \\ -2 \\ \hline \end{array}$ | 15. $\begin{array}{r} 8 \\ -4 \\ \hline \end{array}$ | 16. $\begin{array}{r} 3 \\ -1 \\ \hline \end{array}$ | 17. $\begin{array}{r} 9 \\ -4 \\ \hline \end{array}$ | 18. $\begin{array}{r} 6 \\ -5 \\ \hline \end{array}$ |

## Test Prep

Fill in the ○ for the correct answer. NH means Not Here.

19. Maya has 9 marbles. She gave Pete 3. How many marbles does Maya have left?

6    7    12    NH
○    ○    ○    ○

**Use with text pages 465–468.**

# Fact Families for 11

Complete the fact family.

1.

| 11 | |
|---|---|
| 6 | 5 |

$6 + 5 = \underline{11}$   $11 - 6 = \underline{5}$

$5 + 6 = \underline{11}$   $11 - 5 = \underline{6}$

---

2.

| 9 | |
|---|---|
| 3 | 6 |

$3 + 6 = \underline{\phantom{00}}$   $9 - 3 = \underline{\phantom{00}}$

$6 + 3 = \underline{\phantom{00}}$   $9 - 6 = \underline{\phantom{00}}$

---

3.

| 11 | |
|---|---|
| 8 | 3 |

$8 + 3 = \underline{\phantom{00}}$   $11 - 8 = \underline{\phantom{00}}$

$3 + 8 = \underline{\phantom{00}}$   $11 - 3 = \underline{\phantom{00}}$

---

4.

| 11 | |
|---|---|
| 2 | 9 |

$2 + 9 = \underline{\phantom{00}}$   $11 - 2 = \underline{\phantom{00}}$

$9 + 2 = \underline{\phantom{00}}$   $11 - 9 = \underline{\phantom{00}}$

## Test Prep

Fill in the ○ for the correct answer. NH means Not Here.

5. Complete the fact family.

| 11 | |
|---|---|
| 7 | 4 |

$7 + 4 = 11$   $11 - 7 = 4$

$?$   $11 - 4 = 7$

$3 + 8 = 11$   $2 + 9 = 11$   $4 + 7 = 11$   NH
   ○            ○            ○         ○

**Use with text pages 469–470.**

# Fact Families for 12

Complete the fact family.

1.  | 12 |   |
    |----|---|
    | 9  | 3 |

    $9 + 3 = \underline{12}$   $12 - 9 = \underline{\phantom{00}}$

    $12 - 3 = \underline{\phantom{00}}$   $\underline{\phantom{0}} \bigcirc \underline{\phantom{0}} = \underline{\phantom{0}}$

2.  | 12 |   |
    |----|---|
    | 5  | 7 |

    $5 + 7 = \underline{\phantom{00}}$   $12 - 5 = \underline{\phantom{00}}$

    $7 + 5 = \underline{\phantom{00}}$   $\underline{\phantom{0}} \bigcirc \underline{\phantom{0}} = \underline{\phantom{0}}$

3.  | 11 |   |
    |----|---|
    | 6  | 5 |

    $11 - 6 = \underline{\phantom{00}}$   $11 - 5 = \underline{\phantom{00}}$

    $5 + 6 = \underline{\phantom{00}}$   $\underline{\phantom{0}} \bigcirc \underline{\phantom{0}} = \underline{\phantom{0}}$

## Test Prep

Fill in the ○ for the correct answer. NH means Not Here.

4. Complete the fact family.

| 12 |   |
|----|---|
| 8  | 4 |

$8 + 4 = 12$   $4 + 8 = 12$

$12 - 4 = 8$   ?

$8 - 4 = 4$   $4 + 4 = 8$   $12 - 6 = 6$   NH

○          ○          ○          ○

**Use with text pages 471–472.**

# Names for Numbers

Circle the names for the number.

1. $\boxed{7}$  $\overset{\frown}{5 + 2}$  $3 + 4$  $4 + 2 + 1$

   $12 - 7$  $7 - 2$  $6 + 0 + 2$

2. $\boxed{12}$  $12 - 0$  $3 + 8$  $5 + 3 + 4$

   $2 + 9$  $7 + 5$  $9 + 1 + 1$

3. $\boxed{6}$  $2 + 4$  $12 - 6$  $6 + 0 + 1$

   $3 + 3$  $7 - 2$  $3 + 1 + 2$

4. $\boxed{10}$  $12 - 3$  $9 + 1$  $5 + 5 + 1$

   $3 + 8$  $11 - 1$  $4 + 1 + 5$

## Test Prep

Fill in the ○ for the correct answer. NH means Not Here.

5. Which choice does <u>not</u> name the number $11$?

$8 + 3$      $7 + 4$      $12 - 2$      NH

  ○        ○        ○        ○

**Use with text pages 473–474.**

# Problem Solving:
# Choose the Operation

Add or subtract to solve.

**1.** There are 8 puppies asleep in the basket. Some of the puppies wake up. Now 5 puppies are still sleeping. How many puppies are awake?

_____ puppies are awake.

Draw or write to explain.

**2.** There are 4 gray kittens in the yard. There are 4 orange kittens on the porch. How many kittens are there in both places?

_____ kittens in both places

**Test Prep**

Fill in the ○ for the correct answer. NH means Not Here.

**3.** Ramón sees 9 kittens in the pet shop window. He sees 6 puppies there, too. How many fewer puppies than kittens does Ramón see in the pet shop window?

3      4      5      NH
○      ○      ○      ○

**Use with text pages 475–477.**

Name _____  Date _____

# Activity: Compare and Order Length

Is the object longer or shorter than your hand?
Circle.

1.

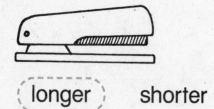

( longer )    shorter

2.

longer    shorter

3.

longer    shorter

4.

longer    shorter

Number the objects in order from shortest to longest.

5.

____    ____    ____    ____

**Test Prep**

Fill in the ○ for the correct answer. NH means Not Here.

6. Which of these items is probably longer than your shoe?

   pen        backpack      bar of soap       NH
    ○            ○              ○              ○

**Use with text pages 499–500.**

Name _____  Date _____

# Nonstandard Units

Choose a unit to measure the length.
Write the measure. Circle the unit.

| Find the object. | Measure | Unit |
|---|---|---|

1.  about _____

2. 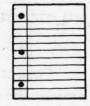 about _____

3.  about _____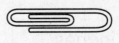

4.  about _____

**Test Prep**

Fill in the ○ for the correct answer. NH means Not Here.

5. Use small paper clips.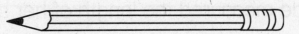

Measure the length of the drawing.

1 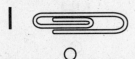    3     4     NH
   ○              ○              ○              ○

**Use with text pages 501–502.**

Name _____  Date _____

# Activity: Inches

Use the picture.
Complete the chart.

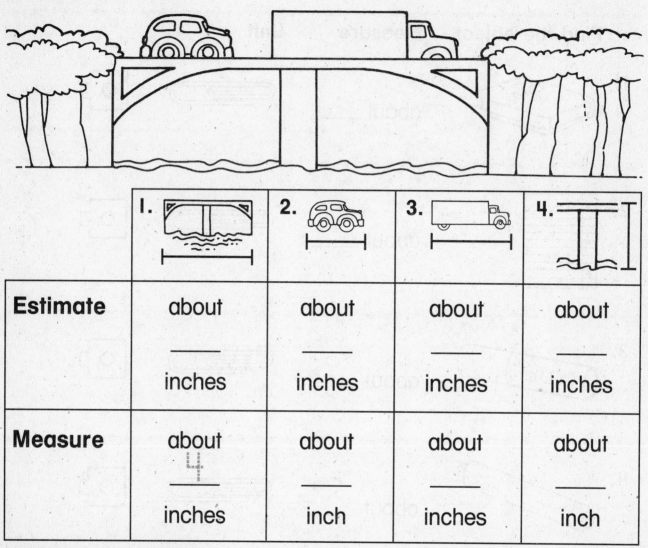

| | 1. | 2. | 3. | 4. |
|---|---|---|---|---|
| **Estimate** | about ___ inches | about ___ inches | about ___ inches | about ___ inches |
| **Measure** | about _4_ inches | about ___ inch | about ___ inches | about ___ inch |

**Test Prep**

Fill in the ○ for the correct answer. NH means Not Here.

5. Jade measured the length of her shoe.
   What is a reasonable measurement?

   2 inches          7 inches          20 inches          NH
     ○                  ○                   ○               ○

**Use with text pages 503–505.**

Name _____ Date _____

# Centimeters

Estimate. Then use a centimeter ruler to measure.

**1.**

Estimate: about _____ centimeters

Measure: about ___10___ centimeters

**2.**

Estimate: about _____ centimeters

Measure: about _____ centimeters

**3.**

Estimate: about _____ centimeters

Measure: about _____ centimeters

**4.**

Estimate: about _____ centimeters

Measure: about _____ centimeters

### Test Prep

Fill in the ○ for the correct answer. NH means Not Here.

**5.** About how long is a pencil?

3 centimeters      15 centimeters      35 centimeters      NH

○               ○               ○               ○

**Use with text pages 507–508.**

Name _____ Date _____

# Activity: Compare Weight

Choose a unit to measure the weight.
Write the measure. Circle the unit.

| **Find the object.** | **Measure** | **Unit** |
|---|---|---|

1.

    about _____    

_____

2.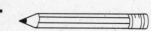

    about _____    

Number the objects in order from lightest to heaviest.

3.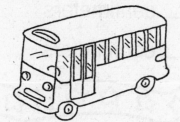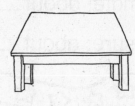

    _____         _____         _____

## Test Prep

Fill in the ○ for the correct answer. NH means Not Here.

4. Kim has a book, a key, and a pencil in her backpack.
   Which is the heaviest?

   book      key      pencil      NH
   
   ○        ○        ○        ○

**Use with text pages 511–512.**

Name _____    Date _____

# Activity: Pounds

Circle.

Use (◯══ Red ══▷ if the object weighs
more than **I** pound.

Use (◯══ Blue ══▷ if the object weighs
less than **I** pound.

1.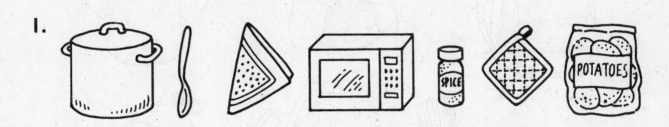

---

**Test Prep**

Fill in the ○ for the correct answer. NH means Not Here.

2. Clare goes shopping.
   Which item weighs about **I** pound?

NH

○          ○          ○          ○

**Use with text pages 513–514.**

Name _____ Date _____

# Activity: Kilograms

Circle.

Use  if the object is more than 1 kilogram.

Use  if the object is less than 1 kilogram.

1.

---

**Test Prep**

Fill in the ○ for the correct answer. NH means Not Here.

2. Which person is about 7 kilograms?

NH

○          ○          ○          ○

**Use with text pages 515–516.**

# Problem Solving:
# Use Logical Reasoning

Solve.

Circle the pencil that matches the clues.

Cross out items to find the answer.

1. It has hearts.

   It is not the longest pencil.

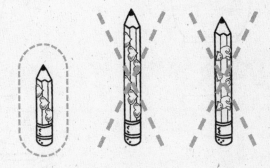

2. It is shorter than the
   dog pencil.
   It has birds.

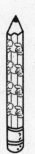  

3. It has stripes.
   It has an eraser.

**Use with text pages 517–518.**

Name _____  Date _____

# Activity: Compare and Order Capacity

Number the objects.
**1** holds the least amount. **3** holds the greatest amount.

1.

_3_  _2_  _1_

2.

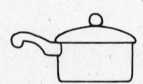    

_____  _____  _____

3.

_____  _____  _____

**Test Prep**

Fill in the ○ for the correct answer. NH means Not Here.

4. Which holds the most?

      **NH**

○  ○  ○  ○

**Use with text pages 525–526.**

Name _____ Date _____

# Activity: Cups, Pints, and Quarts

Use cups, pints, and quarts to compare.
Circle which holds more.

1.

2.

3.

4.

Circle which can hold the same amount.

5.

6.

**Test Prep**

Fill in the ○ for the correct answer. NH means Not Here.

7. Which holds the same amount as these?

            NH

○        ○            ○        ○

**Use with text pages 527–528.**

Name _____ Date _____

# Activity: Liters

Circle.

Use ◖ Green ▷ if the object can hold more than I liter.

Use ◖ Yellow ▷ if the object can hold less than I liter.

1.

Circle the containers that can hold more than I liter.

2.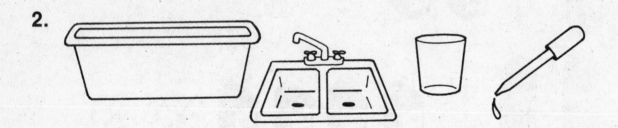

### Test Prep

Fill in the ○ for the correct answer. NH means Not Here.

3. Which holds less than I liter?

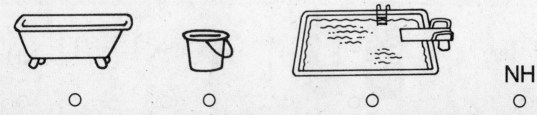

NH

○          ○          ○          ○

Use with text pages 529–531.

Name _____ Date _____

# Temperature

Circle **hot** or **cold** to tell about the temperature.

1. **85** degrees

   ( hot )    cold

2. **30** degrees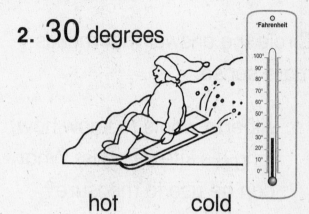

   hot    cold

3. **25** degrees

   hot    cold

4. **95** degrees

   hot    cold

**Test Prep**

Fill in the ○ for the correct answer. NH means Not Here.

5. Which temperature is the coldest?

   **32** degrees    **28** degrees    **35** degrees    **NH**

   ○    ○    ○    ○

**Use with text pages 533–534.**

# Problem Solving:
# Reasonable Answers

Circle the answer that makes
more sense.

1. Alberto wants to know how
   long his kite string is. What
   can he use to measure?

2. Ramona needs to know
   which is lighter, a feather or
   a pencil. What can she use
   to find out?

---

**Test Prep**

Fill in the ○ for the correct answer. NH means not here.

3. Bess has a bag of marbles and
   a baseball. She wants to know
   which is heavier. What can she
   use to find out?

NH

○          ○          ○          ○

**Use with text pages 535–536.**

Name _____ Date _____

# Doubles Plus One

Find the sum.

Think
Use a doubles fact.
Add 1 more.

1.

$5 + 5 = \underline{10}$ | $5 + 6 = \underline{11}$

2. $\begin{array}{r} 5 \\ +5 \\ \hline \end{array}$
3. $\begin{array}{r} 1 \\ +1 \\ \hline \end{array}$
4. $\begin{array}{r} 1 \\ +2 \\ \hline \end{array}$
5. $\begin{array}{r} 5 \\ +6 \\ \hline \end{array}$
6. $\begin{array}{r} 4 \\ +4 \\ \hline \end{array}$
7. $\begin{array}{r} 5 \\ +4 \\ \hline \end{array}$

8. $\begin{array}{r} 7 \\ +7 \\ \hline \end{array}$
9. $\begin{array}{r} 7 \\ +8 \\ \hline \end{array}$
10. $\begin{array}{r} 3 \\ +3 \\ \hline \end{array}$
11. $\begin{array}{r} 4 \\ +3 \\ \hline \end{array}$
12. $\begin{array}{r} 3 \\ +4 \\ \hline \end{array}$
13. $\begin{array}{r} 10 \\ +9 \\ \hline \end{array}$

14. $\begin{array}{r} 9 \\ +9 \\ \hline \end{array}$
15. $\begin{array}{r} 8 \\ +9 \\ \hline \end{array}$
16. $\begin{array}{r} 9 \\ +8 \\ \hline \end{array}$
17. $\begin{array}{r} 4 \\ +5 \\ \hline \end{array}$
18. $\begin{array}{r} 6 \\ +5 \\ \hline \end{array}$
19. $\begin{array}{r} 8 \\ +7 \\ \hline \end{array}$

## Test Prep

20. There are 9 robins in a tree. There are 8 robins on a fence. How many robins are there in all?

_____ robins

Draw or write to explain.

**Use with text pages 557–558.**

Name _____ Date _____

# Add With Ten

Use Workmat 2 and ○. Show the numbers.
Write the number sentence.

1. Show 10. Show 2 more. | 2. Show 10. Show 6 more.

_10_ ( + ) _2_ ( = ) _12_ | ___ ○ ___ ○ ___

3. Show 10. Show 1 more. | 4. Show 10. Show 9 more.

___ ○ ___ ○ ___ | ___ ○ ___ ○ ___

Find the sum.

5.
```
  10
+  4
____
```
6.
```
  10
+  8
____
```
7.
```
   5
+ 10
____
```
8.
```
   1
+ 10
____
```
9.
```
   4
+ 10
____
```

10.
```
   6
+ 10
____
```
11.
```
  10
+  3
____
```
12.
```
  10
+  6
____
```
13.
```
  10
+  5
____
```
14.
```
  10
+  2
____
```

**Test Prep**

Fill in the ○ for the correct answer.

Which number sentence tells about the counters?

15.

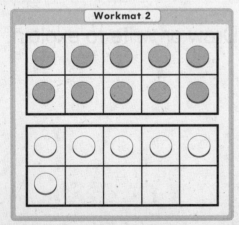

○ 10 + 10 = 20

○ 10 + 6 = 16

○ 10 + 5 = 15

○ 10 + 1 = 11

**Use with text pages 559–560.**

Name _____ Date _____

# Make a Ten to Add

Use Workmat 2 and ◯ .
Make a ten.
Find the sum.

1. Show 8 and 7 more.

   $8 + 7 =$ __15__

2. Show 6 and 8 more.

   $6 + 8 =$ ____

3. Show 9 and 3 more.

   $9 + 3 =$ ____

4. Show 7 and 9 more.

   $7 + 9 =$ ____

Add.

5. $\begin{array}{r} 8 \\ + 8 \\ \hline \end{array}$
6. $\begin{array}{r} 6 \\ + 8 \\ \hline \end{array}$
7. $\begin{array}{r} 9 \\ + 3 \\ \hline \end{array}$
8. $\begin{array}{r} 7 \\ + 9 \\ \hline \end{array}$
9. $\begin{array}{r} 9 \\ + 7 \\ \hline \end{array}$
10. $\begin{array}{r} 4 \\ + 9 \\ \hline \end{array}$

11. $\begin{array}{r} 7 \\ + 6 \\ \hline \end{array}$
12. $\begin{array}{r} 7 \\ + 8 \\ \hline \end{array}$
13. $\begin{array}{r} 3 \\ + 8 \\ \hline \end{array}$
14. $\begin{array}{r} 5 \\ + 9 \\ \hline \end{array}$
15. $\begin{array}{r} 9 \\ + 2 \\ \hline \end{array}$
16. $\begin{array}{r} 7 \\ + 7 \\ \hline \end{array}$

### Test Prep

17. Paul has 8 pennies. Dena has 5 pennies. Make a ten and show how many pennies they have in all.

    Draw or write to explain.

    ____ pennies

**Use with text pages 561–562.**

Name _____ Date _____

# Addition Facts Practice

Choose a way to add.

Find the sum.

> Make a ten.
> Use a doubles
> fact.

1. $6 + 4 = \underline{10}$    2. $9 + 7 = \underline{\phantom{00}}$    3. $5 + 5 = \underline{\phantom{00}}$

4.  $\begin{array}{r} 6 \\ +6 \\ \hline \end{array}$   5.  $\begin{array}{r} 1 \\ +8 \\ \hline \end{array}$   6.  $\begin{array}{r} 10 \\ +2 \\ \hline \end{array}$   7.  $\begin{array}{r} 4 \\ +9 \\ \hline \end{array}$   8.  $\begin{array}{r} 8 \\ +6 \\ \hline \end{array}$   9.  $\begin{array}{r} 3 \\ +2 \\ \hline \end{array}$

10.  $\begin{array}{r} 9 \\ +9 \\ \hline \end{array}$   11.  $\begin{array}{r} 4 \\ +7 \\ \hline \end{array}$   12.  $\begin{array}{r} 2 \\ +8 \\ \hline \end{array}$   13.  $\begin{array}{r} 10 \\ +9 \\ \hline \end{array}$   14.  $\begin{array}{r} 5 \\ +8 \\ \hline \end{array}$   15.  $\begin{array}{r} 5 \\ +9 \\ \hline \end{array}$

16.  $\begin{array}{r} 7 \\ +6 \\ \hline \end{array}$   17.  $\begin{array}{r} 5 \\ +6 \\ \hline \end{array}$   18.  $\begin{array}{r} 7 \\ +5 \\ \hline \end{array}$   19.  $\begin{array}{r} 8 \\ +8 \\ \hline \end{array}$   20.  $\begin{array}{r} 7 \\ +7 \\ \hline \end{array}$   21.  $\begin{array}{r} 8 \\ +7 \\ \hline \end{array}$

## Test Prep

Fill in the ○ for the correct answer.

NH means Not Here.

22. Ben has 9 pieces of a puzzle.

    Dee has the other 6 puzzle pieces.

    How many pieces are in the whole puzzle?

    3 pieces    15 pieces    16 pieces    NH
    ○           ○            ○            ○

**Use with text pages 565–568.**

Name _____  Date _____

# Names for Numbers

Use Workmat 3 and ◯.
Find different names for the number.

**1.**

| Whole |
|:---:|
| 12 |

| Part | Part |
|:---:|:---:|
| 5 | 7 |

| Whole |
|:---:|
| 12 |

| Part | Part |
|:---:|:---:|
|  |  |

| Whole |
|:---:|
| 12 |

| Part | Part |
|:---:|:---:|
|  |  |

| Whole |
|:---:|
| 12 |

| Part | Part |
|:---:|:---:|
|  |  |

**2.**

| Whole |
|:---:|
| 15 |

| Part | Part |
|:---:|:---:|
|  |  |

| Whole |
|:---:|
| 15 |

| Part | Part |
|:---:|:---:|
|  |  |

**3.**

| Whole |
|:---:|
| 14 |

| Part | Part |
|:---:|:---:|
|  |  |

| Whole |
|:---:|
| 14 |

| Part | Part |
|:---:|:---:|
|  |  |

**4.**

| Whole |
|:---:|
| 13 |

| Part | Part |
|:---:|:---:|
|  |  |

| Whole |
|:---:|
| 13 |

| Part | Part |
|:---:|:---:|
|  |  |

**5.**

| Whole |
|:---:|
| 16 |

| Part | Part |
|:---:|:---:|
|  |  |

| Whole |
|:---:|
| 16 |

| Part | Part |
|:---:|:---:|
|  |  |

### ✓ Test Prep

Fill in the ○ for the correct answer.
NH means Not Here.

**6.** Which of these ways will make the sum?

| Whole |
|:---:|
| 18 |

| Part | Part |
|:---:|:---:|
| ? | ? |

1 + 8     8 + 9     9 + 9     NH

○          ○          ○          ○

Use with text pages 569–570.

Name _____ Date _____

# Add Three Numbers

Find the sum.

**Think**
Can I use a doubles fact?
Can I make a ten?

1.  $\begin{array}{r} 8 \\ 8 \\ +\ 1 \\ \hline 17 \end{array}$
2.  $\begin{array}{r} 6 \\ 3 \\ +\ 3 \\ \hline \end{array}$
3.  $\begin{array}{r} 9 \\ 1 \\ +\ 3 \\ \hline \end{array}$
4.  $\begin{array}{r} 4 \\ 9 \\ +\ 4 \\ \hline \end{array}$
5.  $\begin{array}{r} 8 \\ 3 \\ +\ 7 \\ \hline \end{array}$

6.  $\begin{array}{r} 2 \\ 2 \\ +\ 7 \\ \hline \end{array}$
7.  $\begin{array}{r} 6 \\ 4 \\ +\ 5 \\ \hline \end{array}$
8.  $\begin{array}{r} 2 \\ 5 \\ +\ 5 \\ \hline \end{array}$
9.  $\begin{array}{r} 7 \\ 7 \\ +\ 2 \\ \hline \end{array}$
10. $\begin{array}{r} 1 \\ 1 \\ +\ 8 \\ \hline \end{array}$

11. $1 + 9 + 1 =$ _____

12. $2 + 2 + 2 =$ _____

13. $6 + 6 + 4 =$ _____

14. $8 + 5 + 4 =$ _____

## Test Prep

Fill in the ○ for the correct answer.
NH means Not Here.

15. Which doubles fact can you
    use to find the sum?

$\begin{array}{r} 4 \\ 6 \\ +\ 2 \\ \hline \end{array}$

$2 + 2 = 4$   $4 + 4 = 8$   $6 + 6 = 12$   NH
   ○            ○             ○          ○

**Use with text pages 571–572.**

# Write a Number Sentence

Write a number sentence to solve.

1. There are 10 carrot plants in the first row. In the next row there are 9 carrot plants. How many carrot plants are there in all?

   $\underline{10}\;\textcircled{+}\;\underline{9}\;=\;\underline{19}$

   Draw or write to explain.

   _____ plants in all

2. Cindy picks 3 baskets of apples the first day. She picks 4 baskets the next day. She picks 1 basket the third day. How many baskets of apples does she pick?

   ____ ◯ ____ ◯ ____ = ____

   _____ baskets in all

## Test Prep

Fill in the ○ for the correct answer.
NH means Not Here.

3. Meg has 2 bags of plums. Each bag has 7 plums. Which number sentence tells how to find the total number of plums Meg has?

   ○ $2 + 7 = 9$

   ○ $7 - 2 = 5$

   ○ $7 + 7 = 14$

   ○ NH

**Use with text pages 573–575.**

Name _____ Date _____

# Use Doubles to Subtract

Add. Then subtract.

1. $1 + 1 =$ __2__
   $2 - 1 =$ __1__

2. $2 + 2 =$ ___
   $4 - 2 =$ ___

3. $3 + 3 =$ ___
   $6 - 3 =$ ___

4. $4 + 4 =$ ___
   $8 - 4 =$ ___

5. $6 + 6 =$ ___
   $12 - 6 =$ ___

6. $9 + 9 =$ ___
   $18 - 9 =$ ___

7. $8 + 8 =$ ___
   $16 - 8 =$ ___

8. $5 + 5 =$ ___
   $10 - 5 =$ ___

9. $7 + 7 =$ ___
   $14 - 7 =$ ___

10.
$$\begin{array}{r} 1 \\ +1 \\ \hline \end{array} \quad \begin{array}{r} 2 \\ -1 \\ \hline \end{array}$$

11.
$$\begin{array}{r} 2 \\ +2 \\ \hline \end{array} \quad \begin{array}{r} 4 \\ -2 \\ \hline \end{array}$$

12.
$$\begin{array}{r} 4 \\ +4 \\ \hline \end{array} \quad \begin{array}{r} 8 \\ -4 \\ \hline \end{array}$$

13.
$$\begin{array}{r} 5 \\ +5 \\ \hline \end{array} \quad \begin{array}{r} 10 \\ -5 \\ \hline \end{array}$$

14.
$$\begin{array}{r} 7 \\ +7 \\ \hline \end{array} \quad \begin{array}{r} 14 \\ -7 \\ \hline \end{array}$$

15.
$$\begin{array}{r} 10 \\ +10 \\ \hline \end{array} \quad \begin{array}{r} 20 \\ -10 \\ \hline \end{array}$$

**Test Prep**

Solve.

16. Ellen has 16 balloons.
   She gives 8 balloons to Sam.
   How many balloons does Ellen
   have now?

   _____ balloons

Draw or write to explain.

Use with text pages 583–584.

Name ____________________ Date __________

Practice 20.2

# Parts and Wholes

Write the differences.

1\.

| 13 | |
|---|---|
| 9 | ? |

$$\begin{array}{r} 13 \\ -\ 9 \\ \hline 4 \end{array} \quad \begin{array}{r} 13 \\ -\ 4 \\ \hline 9 \end{array}$$

2\.

| 14 | |
|---|---|
| 6 | ? |

$$\begin{array}{r} 14 \\ -\ 6 \\ \hline \end{array} \quad \begin{array}{r} 14 \\ -\ 8 \\ \hline \end{array}$$

3\.

| 12 | |
|---|---|
| 7 | ? |

$$\begin{array}{r} 12 \\ -\ 7 \\ \hline \end{array} \quad \begin{array}{r} 12 \\ -\ 5 \\ \hline \end{array}$$

4\.

| 13 | |
|---|---|
| 5 | ? |

$$\begin{array}{r} 13 \\ -\ 5 \\ \hline \end{array} \quad \begin{array}{r} 13 \\ -\ 8 \\ \hline \end{array}$$

5\.

| 13 | |
|---|---|
| 6 | ? |

$$\begin{array}{r} 13 \\ -\ 6 \\ \hline \end{array} \quad \begin{array}{r} 13 \\ -\ 7 \\ \hline \end{array}$$

6\.

| 12 | |
|---|---|
| 9 | ? |

$$\begin{array}{r} 12 \\ -\ 9 \\ \hline \end{array} \quad \begin{array}{r} 12 \\ -\ 3 \\ \hline \end{array}$$

## Test Prep

Fill in the ○ for the correct answer.

NH means Not Here.

7\. Look at the addition sentence. $7 + 6 = 13$

Choose a related subtraction fact.

| $13 - 7 = 6$ | $13 - 5 = 8$ | $13 - 4 = 9$ | NH |
|---|---|---|---|
| ○ | ○ | ○ | ○ |

Copyright © Houghton Mifflin Company. All rights reserved.

Use with text pages 585–586.

Name _____ Date _____

# Relate Addition and Subtraction Facts

Add.

Then find the difference.

Remember to use
the addition fact to help
you subtract.

1.
$$\begin{array}{r} 8 \\ + 6 \\ \hline 14 \end{array} \qquad \begin{array}{r} 14 \\ - 8 \\ \hline 6 \end{array} \qquad \begin{array}{r} 14 \\ - 6 \\ \hline 8 \end{array}$$

2.
$$\begin{array}{r} 9 \\ + 6 \\ \hline \end{array} \qquad \begin{array}{r} 15 \\ - 9 \\ \hline \end{array} \qquad \begin{array}{r} 15 \\ - 6 \\ \hline \end{array}$$

3.
$$\begin{array}{r} 7 \\ + 6 \\ \hline \end{array} \qquad \begin{array}{r} 13 \\ - 7 \\ \hline \end{array} \qquad \begin{array}{r} 13 \\ - 6 \\ \hline \end{array}$$

4.
$$\begin{array}{r} 8 \\ + 7 \\ \hline \end{array} \qquad \begin{array}{r} 15 \\ - 7 \\ \hline \end{array} \qquad \begin{array}{r} 15 \\ - 8 \\ \hline \end{array}$$

5.
$$\begin{array}{r} 6 \\ + 10 \\ \hline \end{array} \qquad \begin{array}{r} 16 \\ - 6 \\ \hline \end{array} \qquad \begin{array}{r} 16 \\ - 10 \\ \hline \end{array}$$

6.
$$\begin{array}{r} 7 \\ + 9 \\ \hline \end{array} \qquad \begin{array}{r} 16 \\ - 7 \\ \hline \end{array} \qquad \begin{array}{r} 16 \\ - 9 \\ \hline \end{array}$$

**Test Prep**

Fill in the ○ for the correct answer.

NH means Not Here.

7. Kim has 16 pears.

She keeps 7 pears and gives away the rest.

Which tells how many pears Kim gives away?

$9 - 7$    $9 + 7$    $16 - 7$    NH

○             ○             ○             ○

**Use with text pages 587–588.**

# Subtract From 17 Through 20

Subtract.

1.  17
   − 8
   ___
    9

2.  18
   − 10
   ___

3.  20
   − 10
   ___

4.  16
   − 7
   ___

5.  15
   − 6
   ___

6.  17
   − 9
   ___

7.  16
   − 9
   ___

8.  16
   − 8
   ___

9.  14
   − 6
   ___

10.  15
    − 5
    ___

11.  15
    − 8
    ___

12.  16
    − 6
    ___

13.  13
    − 9
    ___

14.  14
    − 9
    ___

15.  17
    − 8
    ___

**Test Prep**

Fill in the ○ for the correct answer.
NH means Not Here.

16. Peter has 19 marbles.
    He gives 9 marbles to Sarah.
    Which sentence tells how many
    marbles Peter has now?

    $19 − 10 = 9$        $19 − 9 = 10$        $10 + 9 = 19$        NH
        ○                    ○                    ○              ○

Use with text pages 591–592.

# Subtraction Facts Practice

Use any strategy.
Find the difference.

1. $17 - 3 =$ ___14___  2. $20 - 10 =$ ___  3. $14 - 6 =$ ___

4. $19 - 8 =$ ___  5. $11 - 7 =$ ___  6. $15 - 4 =$ ___

7. $\begin{array}{r} 16 \\ -\ 9 \\ \hline \end{array}$  8. $\begin{array}{r} 14 \\ -\ 7 \\ \hline \end{array}$  9. $\begin{array}{r} 18 \\ -10 \\ \hline \end{array}$  10. $\begin{array}{r} 13 \\ -9 \\ \hline \end{array}$  11. $\begin{array}{r} 19 \\ -\ 6 \\ \hline \end{array}$  12. $\begin{array}{r} 10 \\ -\ 5 \\ \hline \end{array}$

13. $\begin{array}{r} 17 \\ -\ 7 \\ \hline \end{array}$  14. $\begin{array}{r} 18 \\ -\ 6 \\ \hline \end{array}$  15. $\begin{array}{r} 12 \\ -\ 9 \\ \hline \end{array}$  16. $\begin{array}{r} 16 \\ -8 \\ \hline \end{array}$  17. $\begin{array}{r} 15 \\ -\ 8 \\ \hline \end{array}$  18. $\begin{array}{r} 11 \\ -\ 5 \\ \hline \end{array}$

## Test Prep

Fill in the ○ for the correct answer.
NH means Not Here.

19. Kent has 14 cat treats.
    He gave 9 treats to his cat.
    How many treats are left?

    4      5      6      NH
    ○      ○      ○      ○

**Use with text pages 593–596.**

# Fact Families

Complete the fact family.

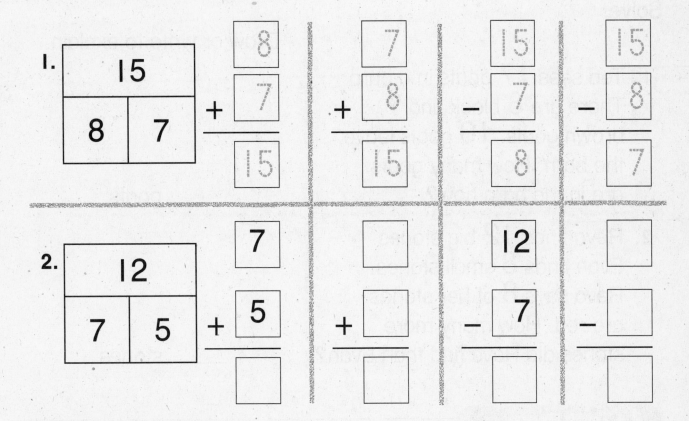

1.

| 15 | |
|----|----|
| 8 | 7 |

$+\begin{array}{c}8\\7\\\hline 15\end{array}$    $+\begin{array}{c}7\\8\\\hline 15\end{array}$    $-\begin{array}{c}15\\7\\\hline 8\end{array}$    $-\begin{array}{c}15\\8\\\hline 7\end{array}$

2.

| 12 | |
|----|----|
| 7 | 5 |

$+\begin{array}{c}7\\5\\\hline\ \end{array}$    $+\begin{array}{c}\ \\\ \\\hline\ \end{array}$    $-\begin{array}{c}12\\7\\\hline\ \end{array}$    $-\begin{array}{c}\ \\\ \\\hline\ \end{array}$

**Test Prep**

Fill in the ○ for the correct answer.

NH means Not Here.

3. Which number sentence
   completes the fact family?

$8 + 7 = 15$          $15 - 7 = 8$          $15 - 8 = 7$

$7 + 6 = 14$        $6 + 9 = 15$        $9 + 6 = 15$        NH

○                    ○                    ○                    ○

**Use with text pages 597–598.**

Name _____ Date _____

# Too Much Information

Cross out the information you do not need.
Solve.

**Draw or write to explain.**

1. Ted sees 17 goats in a barn.
There are 8 black and 9
brown goats. 10 goats leave
the barn. How many goats
are in the barn now?

___7___ goats

2. Reva finds 12 big stones.
Evan finds 8 small stones.
Reva says 8 of her stones
are red. How many more
stones did Reva find than Evan?

_____ stones

### Test Prep

Fill in the ○ for the correct answer.
NH means Not Here.

3. Bob bought 19 goldfish.
10 are orange. The rest are black.
15 are male. How many goldfish are black?

Which information is not needed?

○ 10 goldfish are orange.        ○ 15 goldfish are male.

○ Bob bought 19 goldfish.        ○ NH

**Use with text pages 599–600.**

# Mental Math: Add Tens

Complete the addition sentences.

1.

$3 + 4 = \underline{7}$

$3$ tens $+ 4$ tens $= \underline{7}$ tens

$\underline{30} + \underline{40} = \underline{70}$

2. $1$ ten $+ 4$ tens $= $ _____ tens

_____ $+$ _____ $=$ _____

3. $5$ tens $+ 3$ tens $= $ _____ tens

_____ $+$ _____ $=$ _____

4. $2$ tens $+ 7$ tens $= $ _____ tens

_____ $+$ _____ $=$ _____

5. $4$ tens $+ 5$ tens $= $ _____ tens

_____ $+$ _____ $=$ _____

**Test Prep**

Fill in the ○ for the correct answer.

NH means Not Here.

6. Anya has $40$ pennies. Her mother gives her $10$ more pennies.
   How many pennies does she have now?

   $40$ pennies        $50$ pennies        $60$ pennies        NH

   ○                   ○                   ○                   ○

**Use with text pages 607–608.**

Name _____ Date _____

# Add With Two-Digit Numbers

Use Workmat 5 and ▭▭▭▭▭ and ▱.
Add. Write the sum.

1.
| Tens | Ones |
|------|------|
| 3    | 2    |
| +    | 5    |
| 3    | 7    |

2.
| Tens | Ones |
|------|------|
| 8    | 2    |
| +    | 7    |
|      |      |

3.
| Tens | Ones |
|------|------|
| 6    | 6    |
| +    | 3    |
|      |      |

4.
| Tens | Ones |
|------|------|
| 2    | 4    |
| +    | 4    |
|      |      |

5.
| Tens | Ones |
|------|------|
| 5    | 1    |
| +    | 7    |
|      |      |

6.
| Tens | Ones |
|------|------|
| 7    | 7    |
| +    | 2    |
|      |      |

7.
| Tens | Ones |
|------|------|
| 6    | 2    |
| +    | 3    |
|      |      |

8.
| Tens | Ones |
|------|------|
| 4    | 5    |
| +    | 4    |
|      |      |

## Test Prep

Fill in the ○ for the correct answer.
NH means Not Here.

9. Which exercise is shown
   by these models?

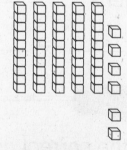

| Tens | Ones |
|------|------|
| 5    | 4    |
| +    | 2    |
|      |      |
○

| Tens | Ones |
|------|------|
| 5    | 0    |
| +    | 6    |
|      |      |
○

| Tens | Ones |
|------|------|
| 5    | 0    |
| +    | 2    |
|      |      |
○

NH
○

Use with text pages 609–610.

# Add Two-Digit Numbers

Use Workmat 5 and ▭▭▭▭ and ▫.
Add. Write the sum.

**1.**

| Tens | Ones |
|------|------|
| 3 | 1 |
| + 1 | 4 |
| | |

**2.**

| Tens | Ones |
|------|------|
| 4 | 5 |
| + 2 | 2 |
| | |

**3.**

| Tens | Ones |
|------|------|
| 1 | 8 |
| + 4 | 1 |
| | |

**4.**

| Tens | Ones |
|------|------|
| 6 | 3 |
| + 2 | 5 |
| | |

**5.**

| Tens | Ones |
|------|------|
| 1 | 7 |
| + 6 | 2 |
| | |

**6.**

| Tens | Ones |
|------|------|
| 2 | 4 |
| + 3 | 3 |
| | |

**7.**

| Tens | Ones |
|------|------|
| 6 | 0 |
| + 1 | 9 |
| | |

**8.**

| Tens | Ones |
|------|------|
| 4 | 6 |
| + 4 | 3 |
| | |

**9.**

| Tens | Ones |
|------|------|
| 1 | 2 |
| + 7 | 6 |
| | |

**10.**

| Tens | Ones |
|------|------|
| 7 | 0 |
| + 2 | 7 |
| | |

**11.**

| Tens | Ones |
|------|------|
| 5 | 2 |
| + 3 | 1 |
| | |

**12.**

| Tens | Ones |
|------|------|
| 5 | 7 |
| + 1 | 1 |
| | |

## Test Prep

Solve.                          Draw or write to explain.

**13.** Molly plays catch for
**23** minutes. Later she plays
catch for **16** minutes. How
many minutes does Molly
play catch in all?

_____ minutes

**Use with text pages 611–612.**

# Different Ways to Add

Choose a way to add.
Write the sum.

**Think**
You can use mental math.
You can use paper and pencil.
You can use a calculator.

1. $\begin{array}{r} 76 \\ +13 \\ \hline \end{array}$
2. $\begin{array}{r} 38 \\ +10 \\ \hline \end{array}$
3. $\begin{array}{r} 74 \\ +12 \\ \hline \end{array}$
4. $\begin{array}{r} 63 \\ +25 \\ \hline \end{array}$

5. $\begin{array}{r} 20 \\ +\ 8 \\ \hline \end{array}$
6. $\begin{array}{r} 16 \\ +\ 3 \\ \hline \end{array}$
7. $\begin{array}{r} 40 \\ +29 \\ \hline \end{array}$
8. $\begin{array}{r} 13 \\ +55 \\ \hline \end{array}$

9. $25 + 4 =$ _____
10. $30 + 10 =$ _____

11. $10 + 25 =$ _____
12. $73 + 5 =$ _____

13. $85 + 4 =$ _____
14. $15 + 60 =$ _____

 **Test Prep**

Fill in the ○ for the correct answer.

NH means Not Here.

15. Roland keeps 32 toy cars in a box.
Jennifer brings 35 toy cars over to Roland's house. How
many toy cars do they have now?

67        35        3        NH
○          ○          ○          ○

**Use with text pages 615–616.**

# Two-Digit Addition Practice

Write the sum.

1.
$$
\begin{array}{r}
14 \\
+11 \\
\hline
25
\end{array}
$$

2.
$$
\begin{array}{r}
50 \\
+23 \\
\hline
\end{array}
$$

3.
$$
\begin{array}{r}
60 \\
+\ 9 \\
\hline
\end{array}
$$

4.
$$
\begin{array}{r}
46 \\
+13 \\
\hline
\end{array}
$$

5.
$$
\begin{array}{r}
76 \\
+22 \\
\hline
\end{array}
$$

6.
$$
\begin{array}{r}
54 \\
+32 \\
\hline
\end{array}
$$

7.
$$
\begin{array}{r}
20 \\
+53 \\
\hline
\end{array}
$$

8.
$$
\begin{array}{r}
44 \\
+43 \\
\hline
\end{array}
$$

9.
$$
\begin{array}{r}
18 \\
+50 \\
\hline
\end{array}
$$

10.
$$
\begin{array}{r}
21 \\
+58 \\
\hline
\end{array}
$$

11.
$$
\begin{array}{r}
80 \\
+14 \\
\hline
\end{array}
$$

12.
$$
\begin{array}{r}
62 \\
+23 \\
\hline
\end{array}
$$

13.
$$
\begin{array}{r}
25 \\
+40 \\
\hline
\end{array}
$$

14.
$$
\begin{array}{r}
36 \\
+21 \\
\hline
\end{array}
$$

15.
$$
\begin{array}{r}
51 \\
+15 \\
\hline
\end{array}
$$

16.
$$
\begin{array}{r}
46 \\
+11 \\
\hline
\end{array}
$$

## Test Prep

Solve.                          Draw or write to explain.

17. The chidren collected
    34 box tops in April. They
    collected 42 box tops in May.
    The children need 70 box tops
    in all. Do they have enough?

**Use with text pages 617–618.**

Name _____ Date _____

# Guess and Check

Use Guess and Check to solve.

| Crayon Boxes | | | |
|---|---|---|---|
| A | B | C | D |
| 12 | 24 | 45 | 52 |

Draw or write to explain.

1. Sophie takes **2** boxes with **57** crayons to her friends. Which **2** boxes does she take?

box _____ and box _____

2. Leando gives away **64** crayons. Which **2** boxes does he give away?

box _____ and box _____

## Test Prep

Fill in the ○ for the correct answer.
NH means Not Here.

3. José and Fredrico want **76** crayons. Which boxes do they want? Use the chart above to solve.

A and B          B and D          C and A          NH
   ○                ○                ○              ○

**Use with text pages 619–621.**

Name _____ Date _____

# Mental Math: Subtract Tens

Complete the subtraction sentences.

1.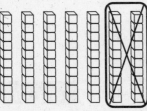

   7 tens – 2 tens = ___5___ tens

   __70__ – __20__ = __50__

2. 9 tens – 6 tens = _____ tens

   90 – 60 = _____

3. 8 tens – 4 tens = _____ tens

   80 – 40 = _____

4. 3 tens – 2 tens = _____ ten

   30 – 20 = _____

## Test Prep

5. There are 50 children in a drawing class. There are 30 children in a pottery class. How many more children are in the drawing class?

   Draw or write to explain.

   _____ more children

Use with text pages 629–630.

Name _____  Date _____

# Subtract With Two-Digit Numbers

Use Workmat 5 with ▭▭▭▭ and ▫ .

Subtract. Write the difference.

1.
| Tens | Ones |
|------|------|
| 1    | 7    |
| −    | 5    |
| 1    | 2    |

2.
| Tens | Ones |
|------|------|
| 2    | 6    |
| −    | 3    |
|      |      |

3.
| Tens | Ones |
|------|------|
| 2    | 9    |
| −    | 5    |
|      |      |

4.
| Tens | Ones |
|------|------|
| 3    | 8    |
| −    | 4    |
|      |      |

5.
| Tens | Ones |
|------|------|
| 3    | 5    |
| −    | 4    |
|      |      |

6.
| Tens | Ones |
|------|------|
| 4    | 6    |
| −    | 5    |
|      |      |

7.
| Tens | Ones |
|------|------|
| 4    | 9    |
| −    | 7    |
|      |      |

8.
| Tens | Ones |
|------|------|
| 5    | 7    |
| −    | 3    |
|      |      |

9.
| Tens | Ones |
|------|------|
| 6    | 8    |
| −    | 6    |
|      |      |

10.
| Tens | Ones |
|------|------|
| 7    | 4    |
| −    | 2    |
|      |      |

11.
| Tens | Ones |
|------|------|
| 8    | 9    |
| −    | 6    |
|      |      |

12.
| Tens | Ones |
|------|------|
| 9    | 9    |
| −    | 7    |
|      |      |

## Test Prep

13. There are 37 children in the school band. 4 children play the tuba. How many children play other instruments in the school band?

Draw or write to explain.

_____ children

Use with text pages 631–632.

# Subtract Two-Digit Numbers

Use Workmat 5 with ▭▭▭ and ⬠ . Subtract.
Write the difference.

**1.**

| Tens | Ones |
|------|------|
| 5 | 6 |
| − 2 | 3 |
| 3 | 3 |

**2.**

| Tens | Ones |
|------|------|
| 4 | 7 |
| − 2 | 2 |
| | |

**3.**

| Tens | Ones |
|------|------|
| 4 | 4 |
| − 1 | 3 |
| | |

**4.**

| Tens | Ones |
|------|------|
| 6 | 9 |
| − 4 | 8 |
| | |

**5.**

| Tens | Ones |
|------|------|
| 5 | 3 |
| − 4 | 1 |
| | |

**6.**

| Tens | Ones |
|------|------|
| 7 | 8 |
| − 1 | 7 |
| | |

**7.**

| Tens | Ones |
|------|------|
| 7 | 7 |
| − 3 | 6 |
| | |

**8.**

| Tens | Ones |
|------|------|
| 6 | 4 |
| − 2 | 2 |
| | |

**9.**

| Tens | Ones |
|------|------|
| 8 | 8 |
| − 3 | 6 |
| | |

**10.**

| Tens | Ones |
|------|------|
| 9 | 6 |
| − 3 | 1 |
| | |

**11.**

| Tens | Ones |
|------|------|
| 8 | 3 |
| − 4 | 2 |
| | |

**12.**

| Tens | Ones |
|------|------|
| 9 | 8 |
| − 2 | 2 |
| | |

## Test Prep

Fill in the ○ for the correct answer.
NH means Not Here.

**13.** A box has 27 apples and 15 pears.
How many more apples than pears
are in the box?

| 4 | 32 | 13 | 12 | NH |
|---|----|----|----|----|
| ○ | ○ | ○ | ○ | ○ |

**Use with text pages 633–634.**

# Different Ways to Subtract

Choose a way to subtract.
Write the difference.

I can use mental math.
I can use paper and pencil.
I can use a calculator.

**1.**

| Tens | Ones |
|------|------|
| 7 | 4 |
| − 3 | 1 |
| 4 | 3 |

**2.**

| Tens | Ones |
|------|------|
| 3 | 8 |
| − | 7 |
| | |

**3.**

| Tens | Ones |
|------|------|
| 9 | 0 |
| − 7 | 0 |
| | |

**4.**

| Tens | Ones |
|------|------|
| 5 | 4 |
| − | 3 |
| | |

**5.**
$$98 - 67$$

**6.**
$$65 - 2$$

**7.**
$$78 - 26$$

**8.**
$$66 - 30$$

**9.**
$$70 - 50$$

**10.**
$$76 - 12$$

**11.**
$$99 - 68$$

**12.**
$$87 - 3$$

13. $80 - 30 =$ _____

14. $42 - 2 =$ _____

15. $46 - 6 =$ _____

16. $73 - 3 =$ _____

## Test Prep

17. Joel finds 10 large stones and
25 small stones. He gives
4 stones to his sister. How
many stones does he have now? _____ stones

Draw or write to explain.

Use with text pages 635–636.

# Two-Digit Subtraction Practice

Write the difference.

1.  $\begin{array}{r} 21 \\ -11 \\ \hline 10 \end{array}$
2.  $\begin{array}{r} 40 \\ -30 \\ \hline \end{array}$
3.  $\begin{array}{r} 58 \\ -32 \\ \hline \end{array}$
4.  $\begin{array}{r} 74 \\ -12 \\ \hline \end{array}$
5.  $\begin{array}{r} 96 \\ -\phantom{0}4 \\ \hline \end{array}$

6.  $\begin{array}{r} 64 \\ -\phantom{0}3 \\ \hline \end{array}$
7.  $\begin{array}{r} 95 \\ -24 \\ \hline \end{array}$
8.  $\begin{array}{r} 55 \\ -33 \\ \hline \end{array}$
9.  $\begin{array}{r} 96 \\ -43 \\ \hline \end{array}$
10. $\begin{array}{r} 26 \\ -14 \\ \hline \end{array}$

11. $\begin{array}{r} 74 \\ -42 \\ \hline \end{array}$
12. $\begin{array}{r} 65 \\ -41 \\ \hline \end{array}$
13. $\begin{array}{r} 86 \\ -35 \\ \hline \end{array}$
14. $\begin{array}{r} 76 \\ -\phantom{0}5 \\ \hline \end{array}$
15. $\begin{array}{r} 49 \\ -\phantom{0}5 \\ \hline \end{array}$

16. $\begin{array}{r} 36 \\ -23 \\ \hline \end{array}$
17. $\begin{array}{r} 54 \\ -33 \\ \hline \end{array}$
18. $\begin{array}{r} 90 \\ -20 \\ \hline \end{array}$
19. $\begin{array}{r} 79 \\ -13 \\ \hline \end{array}$
20. $\begin{array}{r} 87 \\ -45 \\ \hline \end{array}$

## Test Prep

Fill in the ○ for the correct answer.

NH means Not Here.

21. Zack has 33 stickers. His sister
    Kayla has 21 stickers. How many
    more stickers does Zack
    have than Kayla?

    12      14      54      NH
    ○       ○       ○       ○

Use with text pages 639–640.

Practice
22.6

# Check Subtraction

Subtract. Check by adding.

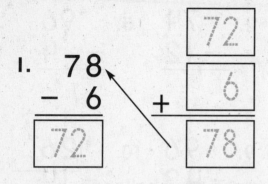

1.   78      +   | 72 |
   –  6          |  6 |
   | 72 |        | 78 |

2.   60      +
   – 10

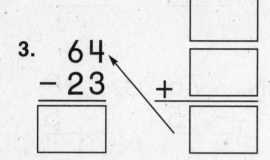

3.   64      +
   – 23

4.   58      +
   – 30

---

### ✓ Test Prep

Fill in the ○ for the correct answer.

NH means Not Here.

5. How many fewer children like grapes than apples?

| Best Fruit Votes | | Total |
|---|---|---|
| Apples |卌 卌 卌 卌 卌 卌 卌 卌 III | 38 |
| Grapes | 卌 卌 卌 卌 卌 卌 III | 28 |
| Oranges | 卌 卌 卌 卌 卌 | 20 |

$38 - 20 = 18$    $38 - 28 = 10$    $28 - 20 = 8$    NH

○                 ○                 ○           ○

Use with text pages 641–642.

Name _____ Date _____

# Choose the Operation

Add or subtract to solve.
Write the number sentence.

1. Sarah has 15 silver balloons and 28 blue balloons. How many more blue balloons are there?

28
⊖ 15
_____
13

13 more blue balloons

2. Jake has 32 baseball cards. Betty has 35 baseball cards. How many baseball cards do they have in all?

◯ ▢
▢
_____
▢

_____ baseball cards in all

3. On Saturday Karen takes 14 pictures. On Sunday she takes 21 pictures. How many pictures does she take on both days?

▢
◯ ▢
_____
▢

_____ pictures

**Test Prep**

4. Larry sees 25 birds at the park. Kendra sees 37 birds. How many more birds does Kendra see?

▢
◯ ▢
_____
▢

_____ more birds

**Use with text pages 643–645.**